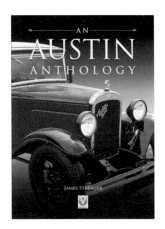

Also from Veloce:

www.veloce.co.uk

First published in February 2018 by Veloce Publishing Limited, Veloce House, Parkway Farm Business Park, Middle Farm Way, Poundbury, Dorchester DT1 3AR, England.
Tel +44 (0)1305 260068 / Fax 01305 250479 / e-mail info@veloce.co.uk / web www.veloce.co.uk or www.velocebooks.com. ISBN: 978-1-787111-91-2; UPC: 6-36847-01191-8.

AN

AUSTIN

ANTHOLOGY

James Stringer

VELOCE

CONTENTS

DEDICATION

I dedicate this book to my wife Avril, who has had to endure my interest in
Austins for over half a century.

Publisher's note
*Illustrating a book of this type is a real challenge, meaning that many of the images supporting the text are of poor quality.
However, we make no apologies for the inclusion of such images as they are of immeasurable importance in terms of enhancing
these stories from the past.*

Foreword

by Bob Wyatt

Austin historian, author of *Lord Austin – The Man* and *The Austin Seven*

When I wrote my Austin history in the 1960s, I was restricted to a single volume of some 300 pages. My research, however, filled a potential second volume, and there was a need to cut out a great deal which was of interest to me – if to no one else! The Austin Seven history was written in haste at that time as it was needed quickly by the editor, the late, great, Bill Boddy. The series never really expanded, but it did take most of the Austin Seven material from my more general Austin Company history.

Several things had to go: further details of that remarkable car, the 1918 Austin 20; munitions production during the Great War; the Cofton Hacket plane factory in WWII; and my own particular favourite, the history of trade union activity at Longbridge – this last subject took two chapters of the book, so it was not used. The only draft went missing when I moved into a smaller house some five years ago – not a great loss though, as the activity of Red Robbo has since been written about by others. The other stories could do with retelling.

Other things were excluded simply because I knew nothing about them and they had not been researched. For the documenting of these, we have to thank Jim Stringer, for so many years the leading light of the Vintage Austin Register, which I had the honour to form with two or three others in 1958. He has unearthed so much of historical interest to the Austin story, and it is so fascinating to have it gathered together here for the first time. We hear about Lord Austin's gentle brother, who Jim brought to light when he was able to interview his daughter; the history of 'Pobble'; an Austin Seven's performance on stage; the Kensitas cars, about which there were legal papers that I saw when I visited a solicitor in Birmingham, but they were lost before I had time to study them – Jim relates the history of the project. Poor Vernon's loss during the war … it always seemed odd to me that he should have been buried near his school in Kent, rather than near his home at Lickey Grange. Jim relates so much else in this volume that will be enjoyed by very many Austin enthusiasts. Enjoy many happy hours with this Austin Anthology.

R J WYATT (MBE)

Introduction

ABOUT THE AUTHOR

I was born in Shepherd's Bush in January 1943, during the time when the Luftwaffe was busy carrying out a bombing raid on London. I was brought home from the hospital a week or so later through the debris-strewn streets of West London in the comfort and safety of a 1935 Austin Taxicab with coachwork by Jones Bros of Westbourne Grove. Thus commenced an instant affection for all things 'Austin.' The taxicab was, of course, owned by a neighbour!

Jim Stringer

When old enough to drive, much to my father's dismay, I purchased a 1929 Austin 16/6 with rare fabric saloon coachwork. Our relationship was not improved upon when, despite being told *not* to put the car in the garage where I lived, I defied my father and almost destroyed the doors at the far end of it, when putting the car away for the first time, having depressed the accelerator pedal instead of the brake. That same Austin still holds pride of place in the Stringer household, even to this day.

On purchasing the Austin for the princely sum of £35, I then became a member of the Vintage Austin Register, and very soon became involved in its running, from initially helping with the first newsletter, to becoming the Hon Sec, then Chairman.

The author's 1929 Austin Sixteen-Six 'fabric' saloon.

I then 'retired,' but two years later took on the job of producing the Register's glossy quarterly magazine, as its editor. Not content with waiting for 'contributions' to be sent in by its members, I started to undertake research into many hitherto untold stories concerning Austin vehicles, aeroplanes, and, of course, the people who purchased them, drove them, flew them, or were simply involved in their manufacture.

So, it is these stories that form the basis of this anthology, added to which are a couple of humorous items taken from contemporary Austin journals.

I have since been granted life membership of the Vintage Austin Register, and am now also the Register's Vice President.

INTRODUCTION TO THE BOOK

Today, the Austin Motor Company is probably only remembered for the Allegro, the Maestro, and perhaps the Mini, and maybe not always for the right reasons. But when the young Herbert Austin decided to break away from Wolseley in 1905, and set up business on his own in Northfield on the outskirts of Birmingham, his one aim was to manufacture the finest motor cars possible, and, to his credit, that is just what he succeeded in doing.

Some of the models that stood out from those of other manufacturers included the Austin Seven, the Austin Twelve-Four, and the London Taxicabs. Today all these models have a strong following of devotees who are determined, through their respective clubs and registers to keep the Austin name alive through the preservation and use of surviving examples.

This work takes a look at just a few of those models, and what their original and subsequent owners did with them. It also takes a look at the aeroplanes that were built at the Austin works during the period of European unrest between 1914 and 1918, and, of course, the people who were involved in their design and manufacture.

The *Austin Anthology* is, as the title suggests, a collection of short stories, some quite short and others considerably longer, which hopefully will provide the reader with an interesting insight into the trials and tribulations of motoring and flying in those far off days, when the internal combustion engine was still in its infancy.

J C (JIM) STRINGER

Herbert Austin looking down into the engine bay of the very first Austin during its final stages of construction. (Courtesy the VAR archive)

Acknowledgements

In compiling this work which covers a few of the lesser known activities of the Austin Motor Company, its products and those who had experience with them I found it sometimes necessary to consult the works of others who have previously touched upon the same subjects. Where the authors of such research is known, their work in this respect is gratefully acknowledged,

Firstly I would like to acknowledge the help and encouragement afforded to me by Austin Historian and Author, Bob Wyatt. For help with the various subjects covered in individual chapters, many thanks also go to:

- Peter Fry for help in compiling the story about Harry Austin, and of course the late Eileen O'Neil, Harry's daughter.
- Carl Coleman, Tony Smallbone and Jack Browne for their help with The Whippet biplane. Also acknowledging the initial research carried out by J N B Collins, and Philip Jarrett.
- Sir Andrew Leggatt and Lynette Beardwood for photographs and help with 'Pobble.'
- John Baker (of austinmemories.com) for the McKenna Duties story, and for asking me to chronicle the events of The Anderson's epic journey around Australia.
- Martin Nutland and Ernie Pease for initial input to the exploits of George Clarke, to Guy Baxter of the Theatre Museum, London, and Ray Don of the Entertainment Artists Benevolent Society.
- The Austin Village Society for information regarding the Longbridge Murder.
- Bob Wyatt and the late Freddie Henry for invaluable help on the Austin Unity Song.
- Bob Wyatt, Ken Bargh, Rob Kentish and Richard Jones (oldclassiccar.com) for assisting in the story on the Kensitas Car.
- The late Bill Manning for his stories about the wedge and the pantomime.
- Les Gammon for the original research into the death of Vernon Austin, and Paul Pollack, the King's School archivist.
- The late Jennifer Hanson for the notes and photographs taken by her great grandmother during her tours around Australia.
- Richard Jones for permission to use photographs of taxicabs, and S Grifford for allowing me to use a photograph from *Desert Taxi*.
- Tony Smallbone and the Rev John Campbell for their contribution towards the essay on the Austrian Alpine Trial.

It should also be acknowledged that articles from both *Austin Magazine* and *The Austin Advocate* are included in this work, and that photographs have been obtained from the same source. Drawings of the Austin Whippet and the Austin-Ball biplanes are acknowledged as being originally published by *Aeroplane* and *Flight* magazines.

Other photographs are either from the author's own collection or submitted with the knowledge and approval of the owners.

J C (JIM) STRINGER

Chapter 1

'Mr Harry' – the other Mr Austin

Together with Peter Fry, President of the New Zealand branch of the Vintage Austin Register, I visited the home of Eileen O'Neal, the daughter of Lord Austin's younger brother, Harry. The following essay about this shy, gentle man was the result of this visit.

Mr Harry Austin in front of the car assembly plant at Longbridge during the late 1950s.

The departure from the scene of Lord Austin in 1941 was seen by many in the British motor industry as the final break in the family link with the company he'd founded 36 years earlier.

It was, of course, an important catalyst for change, heralding the rather less paternalistic regime of the brilliant, but abrasive, Leonard Lord, a renegade from Austin's great rivals at Morris Motors, who was neither loved nor really trusted by the family or workforce.

However, there would remain for another 20 years a benign and calming presence, in the person of Lord Austin's younger brother, Harry, the youngest of six sons of Clara and Giles Austin, born at the family home in 1878.

At Herbert's insistence, Harry was to join his older brother, working alongside him at the Wolseley Company. Although initially reluctant to make such a commitment, as he was on the point of marrying and seriously considering emigrating to Canada, after much soul searching he abandoned any further thoughts of emigration. So began a career with the newly formed Austin Motor Company, an association which would last for the next fifty years, and would see his personal involvement with all the cars which bore the Company name – right up to the Austin Healey, and, of course, the Mini. Like his older brother, Harry never retired.

In 1917, Harry's first and only child, a girl, was born, and it was not long before Eileen became the apple of her father's eye. However, when she was just 12, her mother became seriously ill and died.

Harry with daughter Eileen on the boating lake at Folkestone.

The task of bringing up young Eileen fell to her cousin, Herbert Austin's eldest daughter Irene, who gladly took on the role of surrogate mother, guiding Eileen in all things a young teenage girl in the roaring Twenties should know. They became quite inseparable, and spent many happy hours in each other's company.

Irene had always been fond of Chow-Chow dogs, and was invariably accompanied by one wherever she went. That Eileen also became fond of these strong good-natured oriental animals was inevitable, a fact that did not go unnoticed by her cousin. It was therefore suggested that Eileen might like one of her own. She, of course, agreed, and within a few days a young Chow-Chow pup was being transported by the Great Western Railway to her home – courtesy of her cousin Irene. Such was Eileen's affection for the breed that, when we called on her, she still had one, called Muffin, to keep her company.

Irene was used to getting her own way, and became very emotive when she couldn't. Eileen was once invited to join her as a companion for a holiday, but did not particularly want to go at that time, and told her so. Eileen's refusal was taken as a personal snub, and Irene never spoke to her young cousin again.

During all this time, Harry was working as Production Manager at the Austin Motor Company's Longbridge Works, a position he held for most of his working life. He had many an opportunity for advancing up to director level, but preferred to remain on the shop floor where he was happiest. He would normally start his working day at 8 o'clock in the morning and finish around 6pm. After his evening meal he would often return to the factory from his Northfield home, to see to the night shift.

'Mr Harry,' as he was called, was a quiet gentle man, greatly admired and respected by all those who came into contact with him, but, quite unlike his older brother, he was ill at ease whenever forced into the forefront of attention.

Following Herbert's death in 1941, Mr Harry was expected to fill the vacuum, representing the Company on numerous occasions, a role which he found thoroughly daunting. One such occasion was the Company's Golden Jubilee in 1955, when, under the British Motor Corporation (BMC) banner, he was expected to mark this historic event with a speech. At first he refused point blank, but was eventually browbeaten into agreeing to it. When Harry realised just what he had consented to do, he became 'a bag of nerves,' worrying that he would not be able to do it justice. He would practice his speech over and over again, walking around the house wearing out the carpet and driving everyone crazy with his eternal muttering, as he constantly rehearsed and changed it. When the time came, he not only delivered the speech, but did so with great style and professionalism.

It was around this time that he was asked to appear on the popular BBC radio programme *In Town Tonight,* and again he went to pieces, worrying as to what he should say to the millions of listeners who might be tuned in. He of course did not want to do the broadcast, and it took much persuasion from Eileen and her husband to make him change his mind. When the day came for him to get the train up to London he became almost sick with worry at the daunting prospect which lay before him. However, they need not have worried, as the interview was faultless, and they all breathed a sigh of relief when it was finally over.

That Harry was a great worrier was highlighted when, during the Second World War, the hoarding of foodstuffs was made a criminal offence. Irene had already been caught for hoarding – Eileen recalls there were dustbins full of sugar and dried fruit in the pantry at The Grange, which was also stocked full of all manner of tinned foods.

Harry would not be driven to such measures, and once when he was given two sides of ham, was worried sick that he too would get caught. As a consequence, the offending articles were eaten very promptly.

In the years that Harry worked at Austin, he became involved with most of the vehicles produced, one such being the Austin Seven. By 1935, Eileen was considered old enough to learn to drive, and her father suggested that she may like to have a look on the finishing line to see if there was a car she liked. The one which took her eye was a blue Ruby Saloon, blue being her favourite colour.

The car was duly delivered, and Harry proceeded to teach his daughter how to drive it. The lessons were carried out on the old flying ground at the back of the Works, where other vehicles were seldom encountered. As the flying ground was also used to test new models, there was a steep test hill, and it was here that Harry took his daughter to master her hill-starts, and three-point-turns.

On one occasion, a certain reversing manoeuvre was not going at all well, and the instructor was becoming increasingly annoyed at his pupil's inability to master it. At last, Harry, the most placid of men, lost his patience, got out of the car and slammed the door with such force that it almost tipped over. He then stormed off in the direction of the Works.

The first time Eileen took the car out on her own to show it off to her friends, she nearly wrote it off, when she drove it off the road and into a ditch! However, she eventually proved that she could master the Seven, and became a very proficient driver. When complimented on his daughter's driving prowess, Harry would simply smile and say: "Well, look who taught her."

Eileen with her new Austin Seven Ruby Saloon and Chow-Chow dog.

Eileen came to work at Longbridge during the Second World War as a driver, transporting all manner of motor vehicles from the Works to the railhead for onward shipment to the front. The Works was well camouflaged and only suffered one direct hit from enemy aerial attack.

From the very beginning, Harry was a very loyal supporter of his older brother, and the cars produced by his company. He would never dream of owning anything other

Harry (left) conversing with Leonard Lord at the Golf Club, whilst George Harriman (centre), deputy chairman of BMC, engages in conversation with two other executives.

than an Austin. One day he took his daughter to the London Motor Show, where, in a moment of mischief, she commented favourably on the lines of the new Ford. Harry's reaction was typical, in that he considered the lines of the Ford to be far inferior to those of the latest Austin, and told her so in no uncertain terms.

Throughout his life Harry had but one obsession – golf; he spent whatever spare time he had playing a round or two at the Blackwell Golf Club at Bromsgrove, where he was a respected member. He also organised many of the Works' golfing tournaments, which had become very popular, and an integral part of inter-departmental rivalry between the managers, agents and dealers. Harry's personal handicap remained at a modest 20 right up to the very end.

Going for the hole at Blackwell Golf Course, Bromsgrove.

In 1951, Austin merged with its old rival Morris to form BMC, Harry was not well disposed to the idea, and deeply regretted the demise of the family company.

Harry Austin's death in 1961, from pneumonia, was sincerely mourned by his many friends and colleagues at Longbridge. Aside from marking the end of the family connection with the old company, it was also seen as heralding a new and less settled era in its fortunes.

Harry Austin, relaxing in the garden of his Northfield home.

Chapter 2

The Austin Whippet biplane

It was the First World War that caused the Austin Motor Company to become involved in the manufacture of aeroplanes. Up until that time, Herbert Austin had been quite happy to create some of the finest motor cars available, and to build upon his fast-growing reputation of producing well-built, reliable carriages for the gentry.

With the onset of war, the Government soon realised that if they were to have any chance of coming out on top, they must be able to be aware of their enemy's movements, and the way to do this was by sending up observers in balloons, or overflying their positions with small reconnaissance aeroplanes.

The Royal Aircraft Factory at Farnborough had developed such a plane, designated

An SE5a biplane photographed at Longbridge.

the RE7 (Reconnaissance Experimental No 7), but they alone did not have the capacity to manufacture them in the numbers likely to be required. So, in 1915, companies such as The Austin Motor Company were contracted by the Government to build them under licence. The RE7 was followed by the RE8, of which Austin built 52 of the former and 300 of the latter. However neither plane was considered to be particularly outstanding, and one pilot who flew the RE7 considered it a pig, and so slow that on a windy day it could be overtaken by a boy on a bicycle.

The RE8 was not much better, and was dubbed a 'death trap' and 'an incinerator of pilots' by those who had to fly them.

The third aeroplane to be built at Longbridge was the highly successful SE5 (Scout Experimental No 5), of which 100 were built, and first entered service in April 1917; this was to be followed by 1550 SE5As, which were fitted with a more powerful 200hp Hispano-Suiza engine.

In 1917, the Royal Aircraft Factory's chief designer, John Kenworthy, BSc FRAes, joined Austin as its chief engineer and designer, and soon became instrumental in further developing the Austin Motor Company's capability to design and manufacture its own aircraft, as well as those which were built under Government contract.

In this he was helped by invaluable information on aircraft performance received by the Company from the son of Albert Ball (one of the Company's directors until 1914). Pilot Officer Ball, VC, DSO, MC, provided Austin with many ideas and suggestions as to what would make the perfect fighter aircraft, and when John Kenworthy joined the company, the design of the Austin-Ball fighter AFB-1 (Austin Fighter Biplane) prototype was already well advanced under the direction of Austin's designer C H Brooks.

Sadly, Albert (junior) was never to see his completed biplane, as, at the age of just 20, he died when his SE5 biplane crashed whilst pursuing the brother of Baron Von Richthofen over Annœullin on 7th May 1917 (see Chapter 16 for more on this aircraft).

Although the Austin-Ball fighter was considered to be very successful, only the one prototype was ever built, and it was never put into production.

The AFB-1 was followed by the AFT-3 (the 'Osprey') a single-seater triplane designed to compete against the enemy's outstanding Fokker Triplane, but again, only one prototype was built, as its performance did not prove to be particularly outstanding.

The Austin Motor Company also manufactured just four of the highly successful Bristol F.2B Fighter planes, and John Kenworthy was instrumental in the design of its successor, the Austin Greyhound. However, the first one was not completed until after the armistice was signed, and its first flight was not until May 1919. Only three Greyhounds were ever built.

As the war was drawing to a close, plans were already being drawn up for the Austin Motor Company to build upon its experience of aircraft production to run in parallel with that of motor vehicles. After all, they now had considerable experience in aircraft production, all the necessary facilities, including a purpose-built airfield covering 73 acres, one of the country's top designers, and a workforce of 130 carpenters and 200 riggers and fitters, all highly skilled in the production of aircraft.

Two biplanes were designed by John Kenworthy for the postwar private flyer market, the first being the Kestrel, which was a twin-seater where the passenger sat alongside the pilot, and was powered by a 200hp Beardmore engine. To stimulate

The Austin Greyhound biplane.

interest among the many manufacturers now involved in aircraft production, the Air Ministry arranged an Air Trial at Martlesham airfield near Ipswich, in the August of 1920, and put up £64,000 prize money. Austin decided to enter the Kestrel, which came third in its class, winning £1500. But, because orders were not forthcoming, no further Kestrels were built, and it was eventually broken up.

The aeroplane that came second was the Austin Whippet, a single-seat biplane with the unique feature of folding wings for ease of storage. Five Whippets were built, and put on the market at £500 each, which, at that time, was about the price being asked for a good quality motor car.

The Whippet was a small biplane, with a wingspan of just 21ft 6in, it was 16ft 3in

The front page of the Austin Motor Company's fold-out sales brochure for the Whippet biplane.

long, and just 7ft 6in high, and, with the wings folded, could be accommodated in a garage 18ft long by 8ft wide.

It was first shown to the public at the International Aero Exhibition, held at Olympia in London between 9th-20th July, 1920. *Flight* magazine reported it as being such an easy plane to fly that an experienced pilot could teach anyone to fly one in a very short space of time.

One of the Whippets on display at the International Aero Exhibition held at Olympia, West London, in 1920.

Originally the Whippet was to have been fitted with a two-cylinder horizontally opposed engine, but when it was first flown in 1919, it was found to be severely underpowered. The production version was therefore fitted with a 45hp six-cylinder Anzani air-cooled radial engine, which gave it a maximum speed of 95mph, a climb rate of 5000ft in nine minutes, and two hours flying time.

The prototype Whippet (AU1) was awarded its certificate of airworthiness on 14th July 1919, and was registered to The Austin Motor Company as K-158 (to be changed on 5th December to G-EAGS).

AU1 was flown extensively by the Company's test pilot, Captain Nares, who on one occasion flew it from Longbridge to Bristol, a distance of 90 miles, in just under an hour. A few days later he flew on to Farnborough, a journey which he completed in 55 minutes against a 65mph headwind. It was then flown to Hendon where Capt Nares gave flying demonstrations to prospective customers. The magazine *Aeroplane* reported that an experienced pilot, such as Captain Nares, could land the Whippet on a handkerchief, whilst *Flight* magazine reported that: "Those who wish to demonstrate that their love for flying extends beyond showing off in the company of their best girls might therefore do much worse than consider the Whippet as their next season's sporting mount."

The first purchaser of AU1 was an aircraft dealer/collector by the name of Captain C P B Ogilvie, but there is no record as to what happened to it from then on, other than its registration lapsed on 13th July 1920, and was de-registered in 1931. It is thought that Ogilvie *may* have sold it on to the New Zealand Flying School, although this seems very unlikely.

We do know a little more about the second Whippet, AU2, registered as G-EAPF, in as much that it was flown by H H Sykes from Stag Lane Aerodrome at Edgware during 1923; it was overhauled at Brooklands prior to getting its initial certificate of airworthiness on 17th July 1924, and it was then sold to WW1 flying ace, Flight Lt F O Soden, DFC, who flew it at Gosport on King's Cup Day on 12th August 1924. A year

Prototype Whippet (AU1) – registered 14th July 1919 as K158.

later, he entered the Whippet in the small aeroplane class at the Royal Aero Club's flying contest at Lympne, in Kent, where he took 2nd place. He later delivered it by air in July 1926 to Castle Bromwich, where it was operated by the Midland Aero Club. It was then sold two years later to C R King, a club member, who had it re-engined with a more powerful 60hp Anzani radial engine, before entering it in the Midlands Air Pageant held in June 1928, and the Blackpool Air Pageant the following month. Finally, on 23rd May 1929, it was purchased by a young RAF cadet by the name of Pilot Officer Herbert MacDonald Pearson (later to become Air Commodore Pearson), who paid just £50 for it. By this time it was not looking its best, and needed more than a little cosmetic work before it could be considered fully airworthy. Pearson flew it successfully at around 70mph, down to Calshot where he was stationed, and landed safely in a farmer's field behind the officer's mess. Luckily, he found an empty shed which was an annex to the Flying Boat hangars, where he decided to park the Whippet. However, he was shortly to receive a summons to present himself to the Flight Commander to receive a mild rebuke for planting an aeroplane on property under his jurisdiction without his permission – or indeed any permission at all.

Charles N Gudgeon, a member of the aeroplane design team, demonstrating the width of the Whippet with wings folded.

Pearson was allowed to keep the biplane there, after he had apologised, and then set about replacing the torn and oil-stained fabric. This he had to undertake himself, as permission from higher authority to have it replaced professionally at Calshot's fabric section was not forthcoming.

The next task was to replace the bungee which held the undercarriage together – he found he was in luck when he came across a stock of unused bungee that had been 'condemned' and classified as scrap. After much hard work, the Whippet was ready to fly again, and was towed to where there was a 75ft length of grass and hard standing that would be suitable for take-off. This, he accomplished with yards to spare, arriving at Hamble just ten minutes later. Hangarage here was only available to aircraft with a current airworthy certificate, but the certificate had expired on the Whippet. However, the flying instructor asked Pearson for permission to test fly the biplane to which he agreed. On taxiing for takeoff the 'condemned' bungee broke under stress, and

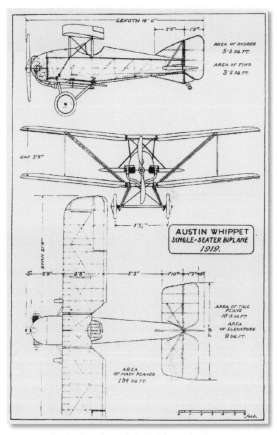

Scale drawing of the Whippet biplane.

the undercarriage collapsed. The flying instructor was far from amused and instructed Pearson to remove his plane from Hamble as soon as possible.

After further repairs and the fitting of new bungee, Pilot Officer Pearson took off from Hamble and headed to Shoreham. Some 20 miles into the flight the engine started to lose power, and he was now desperate to find a field in which to land. After completing a safe landing, he took stock of the situation, and realised that he only had a few shillings in his pocket, and no money in the bank. To make matters worse, he was now in the middle of a field surrounded by curious children asking awkward questions. Half an hour after landing he decided to take a look at the engine, and got it to start at the first swing. Without wasting any more time he took off and was once again airborne, only to lose power again, some 15 minutes later. As RAF Tangmere was nearby he decided to aim for it, and hopefully get his RAF friends to help him fix it. The following weekend the plane arrived at Shoreham without further incident.

Following a thorough inspection by the engineering firm F G Miles, the prognosis was not looking good for the Whippet at all. The report revealed two cracked cylinders

The second Whippet (AU2), registered G-EAPF, at Gosport with engine running.

caused by overheating, and, if that was not bad enough, the Civil Aviation Authority required two of the struts to be sawn through, to check for any rust which may have been inside them. It was also recommended that the fabric on the wings, fuselage and tail plane be renewed. An estimate of over £100 to make G-EAPF airworthy again was far too much for Pilot Officer Pearson, who could not afford to pay for such repairs, and he reluctantly instructed F G Miles of Shoreham, West Sussex to sell it on his behalf. It was sold to a local aeroplane enthusiast for just £15.

Pearson's Whippet, G-EAPF, ended its days in July 1930 strung up outside the Regent Cinema, in Brighton, where it was used to promote Howard Hughes' 1930 film *Hells Angels*, starring Ben Lyon and Jean Harlow.

The third Whippet, AU3, was registered in the UK as G-EAUZ, and then after a short time was sold to a Mr A J Greenshields, who, it is understood, then took it to La Emilia Ballesteros FCCA, Argentina on July 30th 1920, where it was re-registered R-151 and flew until 1928. It was withdrawn from use in 1929.

The fourth and fifth Whippets, AU4 and AU5, both went to New Zealand, imported by Reuben Dexter in the May of 1921, who, as well as running Austin agent Dexter

AU2 ended its days advertising *Hells Angels* outside the Regent Cinema, Brighton. (Courtesy the Mary Evans Picture Library)

Motors (Auckland), was also involved in the New Zealand Flying School. Both biplanes were purchased by Mr Les Brake and W R Bennett, thought to be aeroplane dealers from Wanganui who sold AU4 to Mr H H Shaw, and AU5 to a lady in Christchurch, but there is no record of this latter Whippet ever being registered. We know nothing of this 'lady' but AU5 ended up at The Mirano Brothers' Circus as part of 'The Flying Torpedo' act. Willy and Oscar were balancing artists, and their equipment consisted of a rotating arm balanced on a large scale pylon which was based on the Eiffel Tower. On one end of the arm was mounted a torpedo-like arrangement. One performer sat in the torpedo and operated a motor which drove a propeller. On the other end of the arm the second performer did his balancing act which involved looping the loop while the whole arm rotated

Pamphlet promoting the Mirano Brothers Circus balancing act.

about the pylon at upwards of 90mph. The Whippet had been stripped down to the bare essentials of just fuselage and engine, which was run up noisily to attract the crowds before the performance began, but the plane was not connected to the balancing act in any way. When the circus performers left New Zealand for Australia they took it with them, and the last recorded sighting was in Melbourne in 1929.

On Friday 27th May 1921, AU4, registered ZK-ACR, was flown from Mission Bay, Auckland, to the Ruakura Experimental Farm in Hamilton by a Mr John Seabrook. However, on taking off from a field at Kohimarama, half a mile away from Mission Bay he managed to catch the tail skid on a fence, bringing the little biplane down rather forcibly, and breaking the propeller in the process. By the Monday a new propeller had been fitted, and at 9.25am he took off to complete his journey to Hamilton. In the early 1920s, the only licensed flying field in New Zealand was at Mission Bay, and it was considered to be too short in length for the Whippet.

The mishap was reported in the *Evening Post* of 1st June, 1921, and stated that: "An accident occurred at Kohimarama on Saturday afternoon which prevented the flight of Captain J Seabrook, AFC, by the Austin 'Whippet' machine to Hamilton (says the *Auckland Star*). It was originally intended by Capt Seabrook to start from Epsom, but that not being a registered place under the regulations, he had to go to Kohimarama. The ground did not prove suitable for a starting point for this particular machine. Two drains were safely negotiated, but beyond was a wire fence on some rising ground. It was here that the accident occurred as the machine had not risen sufficiently to clear the fence. The result was a sharp impact, and it was only the fact that an expert was in charge of the machine that the results were not more serious. Captain Seabrook escaped without injury but the propeller and also the rudder of the machine were smashed, thus delaying the journey."

John Seabrook subsequently took off from a beach, to become the first man to fly a Whippet in New Zealand, and the first to fly from Auckland to Hamilton, where he delivered it to a Mr H H Shaw – the first purchaser of a private plane after the end of the First World War. We also know that Mr H H Shaw was the proprietor of one of Hamilton's largest motor businesses, and that it was test flown at the Waikato Winter Show on 5th June 1921 by Sqn Ldr 'Mac' McGregor, who flew over his parent's house situated on the banks of the Waikato River and treated them, and some of the local populace who came out to watch, to a flying display of aerobatics. It was also rumoured *(though proved not to be true)* that he flew the Whippet under the Hamilton road bridge; even though this was unlikely, the rumour persisted for many years. McGregor then made a second flight, only this time over the Hamilton Hospital where a soldier friend of his was recovering from a spinal injury. On landing the biplane Mac confided in a friend that he thought the Whippet was unsafe to fly, being both underpowered and unstable.

In 1924 it was then purchased by racing motorcyclist Percy Roderick Coleman. The biplane was hitched up to his 1918 8hp Perry cycle car which, like the Whippet, had very little power for such a journey, and during the 250 mile drive home several attempts had to be made in order to pull the biplane up some of the steepest hills. Percy was born in 1897, and became involved with motor cars from a very early age, taking up motorbike racing at the age of 14. His passion for flying seemed the next course of action for this speed-loving youngster, who was only 15 when he purchased his first aeroplane in 1912, but never succeeded in getting it to fly – probably just as well, as the only instruction he'd had was from reading about it in a book. However he then took a series of flying lessons at Sockburn aerodrome in Canterbury, after which he purchased the secondhand Whippet.

In an interview published on 22nd August 1964 for the Wanganui Herald, Percy Coleman told the reporter, Phil Hanson, that on purchasing the Whippet, a Mr

Linletter, a member of parliament of the period, made a paddock available on his property for him to fly the biplane. The Whippet was towed to the paddock behind a motor car and test flown by Captain J Findlay, who had earlier taught Percy to fly for £10. The test flight was successful but he bounced the plane on landing. However, he reported that it had flown true, and also that the rigging had been done correctly. When it was Percy's turn to fly the Whippet he found that a strong wind was blowing, so he decided to wait until it calmed down before attempting to take off.

However, the wind did not drop, and Percy climbed into the cockpit anyway and proceeded to take off. After a short time in the air and getting the feel of the controls, he attempted to come into land but found he had approached the landing too fast. He bounced on the ground and back up in the air again, where he attempted

Percy Coleman, owner of AU4.

The Whippet (unregistered), and the
1918 8hp Perry.

AU4 and the 8hp Perry cycle car with which
Percy towed it.

Following his second landing at Foxton Beach,
Percy had to spend the night with his plane to
protect it from being robbed.

A rare photograph of the Whippet in flight,
with Percy at the controls.

to fly round again for a second attempt. He opened up the throttle, but had left it too late and the biplane bounced down, slewed, tore off a tyre and came to an abrupt standstill.

After that inauspicious beginning, Percy spent a lot of time flying around for fun. Heads would turn skyward when the Whippet appeared over Palmerston North doing aerobatics. Percy soon found it rather boring just flying around on his own, so he decided to fly over to Foxton Beach. When he landed, the Whippet had to be roped off to prevent damage by the over-enthusiastic crowd that had by now gathered. But luck was against our intrepid aviator, as during the homeward journey, after being airborne for only a few minutes, the none too reliable Anzani engine started to give trouble, and he was forced to return again to the beach. The whippet was then towed the 23 miles home to Palmerston North behind a motor car.

Sometime later the Whippet flew again, only this time without anyone on board. The engine was started by a friend before Percy had time to get into the cockpit. Unfortunately, the throttle had been left slightly open and as soon as the engine fired up, the biplane took off in a climbing turn, and then side slipped back to the ground. Fortunately the damage was only slight, and confined to the rudder, fuselage, undercarriage and propeller. When the Whippet was repaired, Percy decided to fly to an Anniversary Day motorcycle meeting over at Ashurst, just 6½ miles away. The paddock where the biplane was being kept was covered with large thistles and a single strip had been cleared to enable him to take off. Percy was concerned that he would be taking off into a cross wind, and on takeoff the aircraft was caught by the wind which blew him into some high tension wires, causing it to crash and land upside down. Percy fell out head first, and finally arrived at Ashurst covered in bandages. The incident was reported in *The Press* newspaper of 23rd January, 1925, which had this to say about the incident: "Percy Coleman, the racing motorist and aviator, crashed at the commencement of an aeroplane flight, sustaining cuts and other injuries to his face and mouth. An eyewitness says that the machine left the shed at Milson's line (Palmerston North) and ran along the paddock to take off. The aeroplane rose from the ground to about 20 feet and crashed through the telegraph and electric supply wires."

Upside-down in a field after striking power lines – Percy escaped with only a few scratches to show for this accident.

It was shortly after this incident that Percy decided to part company with the Whippet, and in 1928 put it up for disposal in what can only be described as being in a wrecked state. A Mr W S Dini, who later became the President of the Aviation Historical Society of New Zealand went along to look at it with a view to buying it, repairing and restoring it back to flying condition; however, Percy had already sold the remains to W R Bennett.

It is believed that the Whippet was repaired to the point where it was once again considered airworthy, as it was test-flown at Wanganui in March 1931 by a Mr Les Brake, who, together with W R Bennett had originally purchased the Whippet from Dexter Motors. On 24th October 1932, AU4 was then formally registered as ZK-ACR (eleven years after it was imported) and withdrawn in November 1937. It is known that AU4 only made a few flights during the ownership of W R Bennett, its final flight ending with a forced landing in a turnip field at Kai-Iwi, near Wanganui. It was never inspected for a Certificate of Airworthiness renewal after that, and was put away in the Aero Club's hangar at

AU4, now in the ownership of W R Bennett.

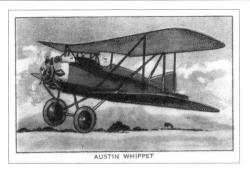

AUSTIN WHIPPET

Cigarette card featuring the Austin Whippet issued by the United Tobacco Company in 1933.

Landguard Bluff Aerodrome 'for much of 1933.'

The last sighting of AU4 was during World War Two, where it was displayed during a War Bonds campaign.

So why did the Austin Motor Company abandon its aircraft division, when there was so much experience and manufacturing capacity there at Longbridge to sustain it? The Kestrel and the Whippet, although excellent aeroplanes, just did not attract the sales envisaged. Other factors which contributed towards its closure was the poor economic situation the country found itself in following four years of war, and finally, although reasonably priced at £500, would-be private flyers found that they could purchase surplus RAF/RFC biplanes for as little as £5 – and who was in charge of the RAF/RFC disposal of surplus fighter planes? Why, John Kenworthy of course!

1. AU1. Prototype registered K-158 was later re-registered G-EAGS. Used by the Austin Motor Company for demonstration purposes. Eventually sold or given to Captain. C P B Ogilvie along with the Kestrel (which may not have been broken up), when Austin ceased aircraft production. Registration cancelled in 1931.
2. AU2. Registered G-EAPF. Re-engined with a 60hp. Anzani engine in 1928. Ended up strung up outside a Brighton cinema, after which it was presumed scrapped in 1931.
3. AU3. Registered G-EAUZ. Shipped over to Argentina and re-registered R-151. Withdrawn from use in 1929.
4. AU4. Sold direct to New Zealand and eventually registered as ZK-ACR. Last sighting was during WW2 when it was displayed at Kai-Iwi during a War Bonds campaign.
5. AU5. Sold direct to New Zealand, Purchased by Mirano Brother's Circus who used it in their fairground balancing act. Never registered. Last seen in Melbourne in 1929.

(Photographs, unless otherwise stated, are reproduced courtesy of Carl Colman, R J Wyatt, or from the author's own collection.)

The author standing next to a full-scale, non-flying replica built by Ken Fern for display at Aero Venture, Doncaster.

Chapter 3
A flight into the unknown

With Britain on the brink of war, and aviation still very much in its infancy, the editor of the August 1914 edition of the *Austin Advocate* magazine chose to print the following humorous account of the Austin Motor Company's Norwich Depot representative Mr Barlow's first (and probably last) flight in an aeroplane. The aeroplane, illustrated below, shows Mr (Bennie) Bentfield C Hucks seated in a 70hp Bleriot monoplane taken during one of his many demonstration flights around the country, and was probably the one in which Mr Barlow took his flight. The following story is Mr Barlow's account of the trip.

A 70hp Bleriot monoplane, similar to that experienced by Mr Barlow. (Courtesy Warwickshire Library website)

"My first experience of flying was rather peculiar. Watching that well-known airman, Mr Hucks, and seeing him take up a lady as a passenger, I questioned him as to the charge required for such a flight. With a few taunts from one or two companions, in less time than I anticipated, I had booked a passage. Once I knew I had to go, the sensation was not at all pleasant, as one suddenly starts thinking about all sorts of things. Taking my seat, and watching the mechanic starting the engine, the usual command 'Let's go' was given, and off we went, running down the course between the spectators. You are most interested in looking at them, and it gives you the sensation of being in a fast car. Upon my first glance down at the earth, I thought we were up a height, whereas we were only about 40 feet up or thereabouts. The next moment I looked straight ahead, when I saw a clump of trees, and my first sensation began. It looked impossible either to get out of the way or pull up, and I already started to cringe down in the seat. You have almost a feeling of terror when sitting behind the driver, and I commenced to curse him as a most reckless devil, when, before I realised what had happened, the machine took a sudden swoop upwards, which was not at all pleasing. We went up, up and up: I thought it would never stop going up, and at last the machine came horizontal. The first turn we made was to the left, and gave me the impression we were going to turn over; but away we went again gradually climbing, and the terrific wind and roar then gave me the idea that the machine must topple over backwards, and nothing could stop it. But by this time I had come to the conclusion that I had got to go through with it, and that I might as well take it calmly – or quietly, as Essex terms it.

"Hundreds of people were looking up, and I thought that a good many were envying me as a passenger, but they little knew as to how I envied them. Everywhere looked either green or brown, and divided into small squares when up so high. Looking down on Norwich, it seems an exceedingly small place, and I expected every minute to be disturbing the pigeons that I knew existed in the Cathedral. Coming back, and flying at a terrific speed, Mr Hucks cut the engine, and after the deafening roar, everything seemed to be dead silent.

Norwich Austin Dealership Manager, Mr Barlow, sitting in the Austin Demonstrator, the new 30hp Vitesse model, which bears the distinctive white diamond on the radiator core.

"What next flew into my mind was whether the magneto had cut itself out or the controls had gone wrong, but the machine gradually pulled up, and dithered just like a bird on the wing, and the next moment we simply dropped about 400 feet.

"The sensation, I can assure you, was about the most horrible that I had ever experienced. At last the engine started off with a buzz, and I felt relieved once more. Then I had my first experience of a bank. This gave me the impression that there was nothing to stop the machine from falling down – sideways. It was then that it occurred to me that Mr Hucks was mad, but after a time I began to worship him, and again was just thinking that I was coming to earth, when away we went up again, and I thought that he never meant to get back to earth. I looked over, but I could not make out where we were, and if a human being was as miserable, or more miserable, then he must be very hard to find. At last I saw people down below. Now I thought my flight was at an end, and wondered whether this marvellous airman would ever have the luck to get down again safely. He seemed to do all the impossible things that it was possible to do. Then I took a look around at what I was sitting on: a few wooden struts and wires, that looked as if the least sudden strain would snap them, and down we should drop as a bird with a clipped wing. I turned around to look at the tail of the machine, and was more frightened than ever.

"Perhaps most passengers desiring to go up do not know the risks entailed, and after several years experience of motoring all sorts of cars – with some very near squeaks. I do not think that there is anything to give you such thrills as having a flight in a monoplane.

"At last we were fairly over the crowd and I saw Mr Hucks look down to the landing place, but away we went again a mile and a half further, then he turned, and took a fearful dive to earth. The next moment we went up again, and made another dive, this process we repeated three times, before the final dive to earth was taken. This sudden rush to earth seemed as if nothing would stop the machine from making a hole in it, and when it started to go up again I was rather relieved. As the sledge touched the ground, the pulling up sensation was similar to that experienced when a couple of tyres are punctured on a car. I was very pleased when the machine stopped, and I did not hesitate many seconds in getting out.

"For quite an hour afterwards, I felt as if I was the 'luckiest dog on earth,' After tea we watched Mr Hucks 'loop the loop,' and I felt very far from comfortable.

"Most people who have had flights and say that they like it, and would gladly go again, evidently do not know the risks they are running, for to say a flying machine is safe is a foolish remark, as that term cannot be applied for a long time to come yet.

"On thinking the matter since, I have come to the conclusion that the people who are fond of flying are not very fond of this earth, or have the utmost desire to get rich quickly; but I do not think that out of all the American millionaires there is one who would persuade me to become a 'Flying Machine' pilot, and if you have the feeling that you would very much like to 'TRY IT,' I say 'DON'T,' or you may regret it before you are very far up."

Based on this account, it is doubtful whether Mr Barlow ever took to the air again!

Chapter 4
An Austin named 'Pobble'

A 1916 illustration showing the transformation
from 'Pobble' the racing car to 'Pobble' the
ambulance.

PART 1: INTRODUCTION

In 1877, sail was still considered to be far superior to the new fledgling steam ships which were beginning to make their mark on the seas and oceans of the world. It was the speed of the square-rigger 'Clipper' ships involved in the Australian wool trade which very much held the key to the success of the operation, with fortunes to be made or lost simply depending upon winds, tides and the skill of their crews in executing a rapid turn-around of the vessels involved.

Cornelius Thompson was very much involved in the design and manufacture of such ships, and after studying at Aberdeen University, joined the family shipbuilding firm of Walter Hood & Company, the building subsidiary of the George Thompson Company of Aberdeen, one of the last operators of these magnificent sailing ships.

In the October of 1877, Cornelius's second wife Agnes Marion Williamson, gave birth to their third and final child, a boy, whom they christened Oscar Stephen. Their first son, Walter, was born in 1873, then a daughter, Muriel Annie, was born in 1875. All three children grew up in the strictly controlled environment of a wealthy Victorian Scottish family, where money was able to provide all the luxuries available at that time.

Cornelius died at the relatively young age of 50, on the 18th January 1894, on board the *Damascus*, which was just two days out from London and bound for Australia. Shortly afterwards, his widow moved down to London with Walter, Oscar and Muriel, and took up residence at 48, Queen's Gate, in fashionable South Kensington. Oscar had been sent down to Kent some years earlier to be educated at Tonbridge School, and in 1894 at the age of 22, he entered the London Office of George Thompson & Company, where he was made a partner. His flair for designing ships was put to good use when he became involved in the planning of the later generation of steam ships for the Aberdeen White Star Line. Muriel was educated at Blackheath High School and Hacking College, in North London, and as well as taking an interest in motor cars she also became involved in the Suffragette movement. Walter however, was a chess enthusiast and specialised in the composition and solution of chess problems.

By this time, steam was replacing sail on the high seas, and the motor car, which was replacing the horse, was beginning to make its mark on the roads and highways around the civilised world, a fact which had not gone unnoticed by the three siblings who took more than just a passing interest in this new and exciting mode of transport. Very quickly a variety of motor cars had been purchased, and then driven at speeds often in excess of the recognised limits imposed under the notorious 'Red Flag Act.'

On one such occasion in July 1905, the motor car which Oscar was driving caught fire with disastrous effect, and was reported thus in a local West London newspaper under the heading 'MOTOR CAR ON FIRE.' The report described how a motor car belonging to Mr Oscar Thompson, of 48, Queen's Gate, caught fire in Bridge Road (Hammersmith). "On Tuesday evening, becoming well alight within a few moments". The reporter then went on to say that: "mould (earth/soil) from a nearby garden was dumped on the flames, which, together with the arrival of the Fire Brigade added to the excitement of the large crowd which by this time had gathered". The report concluded by saying that: "The car, a 'new one', was almost totally wrecked in the flames, and the owner was severely bruised (burned?) about the hands. Two ladies who were riding in the car were also slightly burned, and being considerably alarmed sought refuge in a nearby house from whence they were conveyed home in a cab."

The report does not indicate what make of motor car it was, but from various reports we have, we know that around the time of the incident, one of the following could have been involved: An 8.1hp Wolseley, a Siddeley (which may have been the Wolseley) 6.5hp Austin, or a 30hp Daimler.

PART 2: THE THIRST FOR SPEED
It was the 30 horse power Daimler that Oscar entered for the Edmund's Trophy at Blackdown Park in 1906, and which earned him the dubious reputation (if the following report was anything to go by) of being a little on the reckless side of careful.

"Mr Oscar Thompson, last on the programme, undoubtedly gave the best 'show,' for dashing up to the bend in a veritable tornado of dust and small stones, his car charged right off the road onto the grass, the off-side front tyre bursting at the same time with a loud report. Nevertheless by great exertions he avoided hitting the flags which marked the extreme limits of the course, and he got back again onto the road, finishing the rest of the hill with a deflated tyre". The report continued: "Mr Oscar Thompson once more caused a thrill of excitement by taking the turn so short that both the outside wheels lifted clear of the ground and the car appeared to be in imminent risk of capsizing. However this was happily just avoided but it was a narrow shave." The report concluded: "The last car was again Mr Thompson, and this being the third time, there was a noticeable move by the spectators to get away to a respectable distance. Unfortunately, owing to commutator trouble, the owner was obliged to give up after getting half way through the course."

Oscar's 'devil-may-care' attitude to motor racing was matched only by that of his sister, Muriel, whose attitude to life was demonstrated by her exploits on the track and, several years later, in the battlefields of France. Muriel, as stated earlier, was also involved, and indeed a founder member of the Suffragette movement. Because of her ability to drive, she was engaged as chauffeur to Miss Emily Pankhurst for the Women's Social & Political Union (WSPU), so it should come as no surprise that this feisty lady was one of the advocates of equal rights for women.

By now Oscar had purchased a property in Kensington, where he intended to concentrate all his efforts into running the London end of the business, and for good measure he became a member of the Bath Club, the fledgling Royal Automobile Association, and, with his brother Walter, also helped to establish the Brooklands' Automobile Racing Club, of which they both became founder members.

Such was his interest in the automobile, that when the Brooklands race track opened at Weybridge in 1905, Oscar was one of the first to try it out, and as a founder member was able to use the track to put his motor cars through their paces.

Muriel had also developed an insatiable appetite for speed, and was often to be seen at Brooklands either in the company of Oscar or their brother Walter, inevitably behind the wheel of a fast motor car.

PART 3: 'POBBLE' IS BORN

The reasons behind Oscar's decision to buy an Austin will probably never really be known, but he could very well have been impressed by the 25/30 Austin touring car that gained an enviable reputation for reliability by running without any mechanical faults, other than a broken chain sprocket, for four days whilst participating in the very hilly Scottish trial in June 1906. The course was from Glasgow to Glasgow via Moffat, Edinburgh, Perth, Aberdeen, Keith, Grantown, Pitlochry, and Inveraray.

Oscar took delivery of his Austin on 8th June, 1907, shortly after an identical model was timed climbing up a hill at Shelsley in Warwickshire at 2 minutes, 25.8 seconds.

Both he and his sister were very

An Austin advertisement outlining recent successes with their motor cars, which may have influenced Oscar to purchase 'Pobble.'

pleased with their purchase, which they named 'Pobble' after the Edward Lear nonsense-verse character "The Pobble who has no toes." The reason for this was never recorded, and will probably never be known.

The Austin 25/30 was the first to be produced by the Austin Motor Company in any quantity. Its four-cylinder engine had a bore and stroke of 120 x 127mm which developed 32bhp at 900rpm, and was mounted on a 9ft 9in wheelbase chassis with 9in ground clearance. The final drive was by live rear axle, rather than chain as fitted to the Scottish and Shelsley trial cars.

Following registration in the County of Lanark, and now sporting the number V33, Oscar and Muriel began using the car for touring, covering a distance in excess of 10,000 miles in just under eight months, which, considering the condition of the roads at that time was no mean feat. Satisfied with the construction and reliability of the Austin, Oscar decided that this was the car with which he could now attempt to conquer Brooklands.

The original engine was replaced on 27th February, 1908, with a new 40hp unit with 121 x 127mm bore and stroke (5824cc). It also had an especially large carburettor and had different gear ratios fitted in the gearbox. The standard 'tourer' body was replaced with a special lightweight two-seater one, which was subsequently copied by the Austin Motor Company, and featured in its 1909 catalogue as 'The Brooklands' model.

Pobble's first rather inauspicious appearance at Brooklands was on 18th April 1908, when Oscar entered it in the fourth race of the day; clearly this was not a momentous beginning, as the car, whilst finishing, was not placed.

Better luck was to follow when he came in first during the third race on 9th May, but later, in race 8 he was once again 'not placed.' On May 12th Oscar Thompson challenged H G Nalder to a private race at Brooklands over a distance of 5 miles. Nalder was driving a 35.7hp Berliet. The two cars raced around the course neck and neck for practically the whole distance, but Nalder was able to creep a length ahead just as the winning post was reached.

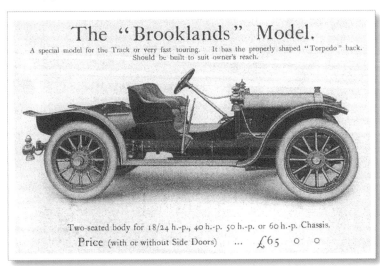

The "Brooklands" Model.

A special model for the Track or very fast touring. It has the properly shaped "Torpedo" back. Should be built to suit owner's reach.

Two-seated body for 18/24 h.-p., 40 h.-p. 50 h.-p. or 60 h.-p. Chassis.

Price (with or without Side Doors) ... £65 o o

The Austin 'Brooklands' Model, no doubt inspired by the success of the 25/30 car, purchased by Oscar Thompson (from a 1909 Austin catalogue).

The following month Oscar entered the car in the third heat of the President's handicap, where after averaging 70mph he gained first place, but unfortunately the car failed to gain him a place in the final. It is perhaps noteworthy to record that also on this day, 8th June, the 100hp Grand Prix Austins were to be given their first official airing at a special event which was organised to take place at Brooklands.

On 4th July, Oscar's sister Muriel entered Pobble in the ladies' handicap race, which was the first ladies' race to be held at Brooklands. The following report was published in *The Car*, dated 8th July, 1908, and gives a good insight to the event.

"A bright afternoon favoured the Brooklands races on Saturday, though the bad morning, to a great extent, must have deterred many intending spectators from being present at this meeting. The half-crown enclosure was very poorly patronised, and the paddock was not inconveniently crowded at any time; in fact, one may be quite safe in saying that 2500 was a very liberal estimate of the number of people in attendance. The car enclosures also, both members' and public, were not by any means full. It was unfortunate that several of the proposed races failed to fill, so that no really important events appeared on the programme. The chief centres of interest were the Ladies' Bracelet Handicap and the private match between Messrs Stocks and Edge. This latter event proved to be the best and most interesting of the day, the final issue being uncertain all through the race and the finish being very close place. Victory however, falling to the latter by a few yards only. The other events can be classed as fairly interesting, nothing of note and no really exciting finishes being witnessed".

The tone of this report would certainly seem to suggest that motor racing, though still in its infancy, was considered to be very much a 'male' dominated preserve, and that the women's event was not taken at all seriously. The race, however, was won by Muriel Thompson at an average speed of 50mph over a distance of 5¾ miles.

Muriel Thompson at the wheel, Oscar standing to the right at Brooklands in 1907.

Pobble was entered for four events during August 1908. On 3rd August, Oscar came third in the first race, but in the third race the car was driven by Muriel. She competed against Mrs Christabel Ellis, driving an Arrol-Johnston called 'Guarded Flame,' and Mrs Ethel Locke King, the wife of the Brooklands track owner Hugh Fortescue Locke King, who drove an Itala called 'Bambo.' Following a tense and exciting race, Muriel Thompson beat the competition, and Pobble came in first at over 50mph.

Pobble in early pre-streamline guise.

Pobble soon became recognised as a 'regular' and worthy competitor at Brooklands, and between 1908 and 1909 participated in over 36 events, collecting eleven firsts, six seconds and six thirds. During this time, the Austin's specification remained largely unaltered, although during 1909 the top gear ratio was increased to 2.36:1, and with fine-tuning to the engine, its average speed was able to be increased from 67mph to 71mph, and later increased again to 81mph. It is worth noting that in 1911 the car was recorded as being lapped at a staggering 91mph, although it has to be said that on this occasion a lighter more streamlined body had been fitted.

With careful tuning Pobble could now consistently achieve high speeds, but because of the unmodified suspension, it became difficult to control. However, 1909 was to be regarded as Pobble's finest year for competitions.

Whilst Pobble spent most of its competitive life at Brooklands, in July 1909 Oscar entered it in the Shelsley Walsh Hill Climb. The car was driven by Syd Hands, who ascended Shelsley in one minute 25 seconds, the fastest time of the day.

In August, Oscar entered Pobble in the Senior Private Competitor's Handicap at Brooklands. The race was between him and Sir George Abercrombie who was driving a Napier, and thirteen other competitors, and was held over a distance of 8½ miles. Pobble soon took the lead from the other 14 competitors, which Oscar held right to the commencement of the finishing straight when Sir George began to pull even and overtake. Just as the crowd thought that Pobble would lose the race, the Napier began to lose speed and Thompson crossed the line, winning by 30 yards. The explanation for the loss of speed being that the Napier had broken an ignition cable at the critical moment and the engine had died, the

Brooklands, 1909. Opening the paddock gates, then rushing back to her car – all as part of the obstacle race and hillclimb, which, of course she won.

Muriel preparing to take part in the blindfold driving test, which again she won outright.

Now in streamline trim at Brooklands.

Muriel in Pobble with her nephew, who, at the age of 16, joined the Royal Navy, attained the rank of Captain, and was also awarded the DSO for bravery. (Courtesy Lynette Beardwood)

car crossing the line under its own momentum. Pobble's average speed for the handicap was 61.5mph.

Later, in the Senior Handicap, Oscar Thompson was able to push that average up to 69.7mph and finish first with a clear lead of 300 yards against Sir George's Napier.

By 1910, Pobble had now become something of a legend and continued to enjoy success after success at the Brooklands track. Such success was typified by the result of the June Invitation Race, which saw the Vauxhall driven by Bashall take the lead as soon as the flag was dropped. Pobble soon caught up with the Vauxhall, and gradually pushed in front. There then followed a duel between the two vehicles, which only ended when the Vauxhall had the misfortune to break a petrol pipe. Pobble continued in the lead with E H Turnbull in his Bleriot just 3⅖ seconds behind him and another Bleriot just 2⅖ seconds away from him. The three drivers maintained this position until the very end, when Pobble entered the finishing straight 150 yards ahead of Turnbull. However with the finish line in sight, Pobble began to slow and although finishing first, Turnbull's Bleriot flashed into second place just one second behind him.

In July, Thompson again entered Pobble in the Shelsley Walsh Hill Climb, and took the car up the tortuous route in a remarkable 1 minute, 10⅔ seconds, which again turned out to be the fastest time of the day, having beaten at least two six-cylinder cars with bores of 124mm and 127mm, respectively.

At the conclusion of the 1910 season, Oscar Thompson announced that Pobble was to retire from the race track, and was unlikely to ever race again, but the following year the Austin was back in action again, and in August 1912 Muriel drove the car in what was to be its last competitive event: 'The Royal Automobile and Associated Club's Gala Day and Hill Climb'. *Autocar*, on 3rd August 1912, reported the event under the heading 'The Skilful Driving Race and Hill Climb,' stating that "Miss Muriel Thompson's superb handling of the veteran Austin, 'Pobble,' seemed to mark her as a likely winner, but she failed in the Motor House" (ie, the garage parking test).

The Auto on the other hand reported the day's events as follows:

"A great success was scored by the organisers of the inter-club meeting at Brooklands on Saturday, and it has been shown conclusively enough that there is ample room in automobile calendar for amateur events of this kind. The track wore a quite unwanted aspect, and nothing could have been more interesting than the presence of genuine touring cars in large numbers being driven in sporting fashion by private owners. Of course a certain number of what are practically racing vehicles managed to work their way into the competition and it would be difficult, indeed to know how to keep them out so long as the drivers in their private capacity are members of associated clubs; generally speaking, however, the entries were of a strictly amateur type. The sport provided was mostly good while nothing more amusing in the way of gymkhana events has ever been seen than the blindfold competition. To the majority of the competitors in this event it must have been a revelation to find, when the bandage was removed from their eyes, how hopelessly at fault they had been in their calculations; on the other hand, Miss Muriel Thompson drove with almost as much confidence and precision as though she had been able to see, and was the only one to reach the finishing line. By comparison with the entire failure of the other competitors it will always be a source of wonderment to the spectators how this skilful sportswoman managed to make the feat look so ridiculously easy, whilst an unknown correspondent chose to write more on the re-appearance of the now 'retired' Pobble at Brooklands.

"We bade farewell to 'Pobble' last week, and did not know we were to meet the same car again so soon as Saturday. It looked somewhat sobered with the addition of a touring body, but still with the sporting disc wheels, the spats of the modern racing car. Skilfully piloted by Miss Thompson, the car secured for her the first prize in the Declaration Handicap, and in the Blindfold Competition."

The Standard, however, had this to say on the event: "The rest of the programme was alright, if a little heavy, as such things as obstacle, skilful driving, blindfold competitions ought to be treated in a spirit of supreme gaiety, and all club haughtiness and provincial propriety laid aside. The racing proper on the old Brooklands' lines was much the same as usual, and produced many of the same cars and drivers, habitués of the track; and one person who shone by skill was Miss Muriel Thompson, who was driving the famous old 'Pobble,' the 'Dean Swift' of the track, disguised by the touring body, but wearing the wheels of a wicked past. Both the other two inter-club events, the hill climb and the relay race were won by the Tykes, who were what we call in the vernacular 'hot stuff' – Hubert Wood's Crossley and Kidner's Vauxhall, Coatalen's Sunbeam and Kirk's Talbot – Arcades ambo twice over, and so it came and passed, this meeting of the clans, with its promises fulfilled and unfulfilled, its faults and its failings, its good points and its bad. It is not wise to be too severe upon the initial indiscretions. Hope is one of our proverbial chest troubles, like tuberculosis. The future may bring forth a great mustard tree from the last Saturday's seed, sown though it were upon cement."

Two interesting views of Austin " Pobble " in racing trim and in mufti.

The interesting characteristics of this car are: Bore and stroke 120 mm. by 127 mm., gear ratio 2.36, 19-tooth pinion into 45-tooth wheel, road wheels are 820 by 120 all round, ground clearance is a little over 9in. The car was first built as a 25-30 h.p. with an 18-24 h.p. gear box, and was delivered on June 8th, 1907. The engine was taken out on February 27th, 1908, and a 40 h.p. engine put in its place, since which date the car has undergone no radical changes. Two new pistons were fitted, the original ones being cracked during racing, and a few months ago white metal crankshaft bearings replaced the phosphor bronze ones as they stand excessive engine speed better. The gear ratio of the back axle has been changed two or three times, as, of course, the ratio for Brooklands is hardly suitable for hill-climbing. With the exception of these parts the car has had no alteration from standard, so that, when it is taken into consideration that the car has toured 30,000 miles, in addition to its racing exploits, its record is really remarkable.

A newspaper cutting showing Pobble in racing trim and as a normal touring car at the end of its racing career.

Winning Post covered much the same as *The Standard*, but ended its piece by having a slight knock at the then quite young RAC, when it commented: "Apart from this, there was some ordinary racing at Brooklands' with many familiar cars and drivers, lightened by blindfold, obstacle and skilful driving competitions, The RAC fairly coming off its perch of dignity and frivolling in cap and bells – and no bad thing either for a change. Dulce est desipere, you know, even in the very best set. Frankly, apart from the one portentous fizzle, the show was quite a success, and must be repeated annually to bring the clubs and associates into close touch. One of the notable features of the afternoon was the clever driving of Miss Muriel Thompson, own niece to 'Pobble'."

Although Oscar Thompson entered Pobble once more in the first race on 25th September, there was no record of him actually taking part in the event.

The five years in which Pobble dominated the race track at Brooklands were not only a credit to the skill, luck and fortitude of Oscar and Muriel Thompson, but also to the designer and manufacturer of this quite remarkable Austin Motor Car.

As an interesting aside, it is worth mentioning a comment published in 1912, when Pobble had finally 'retired' from racing and been refitted with a landaulet body, and was in Cornwall on a 'family outing'. The article reads thus: "After finishing its racing career in August this year it had its ordinary carriage body replaced and the family were touring with it in Cornwall. Garaging one night in a wayside hotel, another motor car arrived and was duly placed alongside. "Well, you have a cheek," said the chauffeur of the new arrival. "To call your car 'POBBLE,' don't you know it is the name of a famous racing car?" he cried to the mechanic attached to it. When the explanation was given that it was Pobble, the collapse of the chauffeur was amusing to the beholders, and perhaps the best testimony to the all-round qualities of Austin cars yet given. But to return to Pobble's speed: in April this year it averaged sixty-eight miles per hour. In June it had increased this to eighty-seven miles per hour, which only shows how the same engine, chassis &c can be improved by judicious tuning-up."

PART 4: POBBLE GOES TO WAR

"Brooklands racegoers of a few years ago will remember Pobble, a car that distinguished itself during several seasons. It was, and is the property of Mr Oscar S Thompson, a well-known member of the RAC. This splendid old car is now serving as an ambulance with the French troops in the Vosges district. Mr Thompson having joined the British Ambulance Committee that is working under the French Military Authorities in those mountainous regions. Undoubtably the car and its driver are finding plenty of strenuous work to do in helping our gallant allies. During the last three months Mr Thompson has, we are informed, carried between 300 and 400 wounded men, and had driven more than a thousand miles. Most of the driving has to be done at night and no lights are allowed." Thus was Pobble's transformation from racing car to ambulance reported in one of the contemporary motoring journals.

Pobble had barely time to become accustomed to the more relaxed pace of retirement when an Archduke from an obscure Baltic State was assassinated, which, as events were to show, caused the whole world to be thrown together in what we now know as the First World War. The British Government, with a rare but inspired moment of foresight, considered that it was highly likely that a vast number of mechanised ambulances would be needed to cope with the casualties that would inevitably occur.

A call via the motoring organisations went out to the owners of motor cars, to donate not only their vehicles but their drivers too, brought hundreds of vehicles of all shape, sizes and makes to the depots which were set up to receive them.

Oscar Thompson was one of those owners who decided that patriotism came before personal need, and offered Pobble, himself and Thomas Holdstock, his chauffeur to aid the war effort.

So once again Pobble was subjected to a change of coachwork, only this time the body style was to be that of an ambulance, but along each side, just beneath the distinctive Red Cross, was attached a pennant displaying the name 'Pobble' as a reminder of its association with another more carefree era.

Oscar joined one of the several volunteer ambulance convoys organised by the French Red Cross, and took Pobble over to France with him. Muriel also wanted to play her part, but was advised by the authorities that women were not welcome. Not to be

Now converted to an ambulance, but still sporting a pennant upon which its name is proudly displayed, ready to do service across the channel.

thwarted by petty officialdom, Muriel joined the First Aid Nursing Yeomanry (FANY), which in 1914 had been quick to adopt mechanised transport. However, their services had been refused by the British, so they assisted the French and Belgian armies instead.

Muriel left England for Calais on 18th February, 1915, and took up her post in a Belgian military hospital at Lamark. By the end of March she was personally decorated with the Chevalier de l'Order de Leopold II by the Belgian King at La Panne, for evacuating wounded Belgian soldiers under fire.

Nearer to the German border in Alsace, the fighting around Vosges had been fierce, and several big engagements were encountered, the ambulance units which

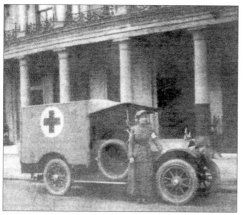

Left: Muriel with 'Unity' the Unic ambulance that was assigned to her for the duration of the war. Below: in France with Unity.

Wearing the Chevalier of the Order of Leopold II, personally presented to her in the field on 29th March 1915 by His Majesty King Albert (of the Belgians) for evacuating wounded Belgian soldiers under fire near Dixmude.

had been sent over from England as part of sections 1 and 2 of the British Ambulance Committee were kept fully occupied with scarcely time to service and repair the vehicles. Early in July 1914, the battle of La Fontenelle subsided, and the ambulance section was able to retire to its original base for a refit. The French were so satisfied with the first two convoys that they asked if more could be supplied.

Oscar, together with Thomas Holdstock and Pobble were assigned to Section 3 of the British Ambulance Committee, which, before starting their journey from Southampton on 6th February 1915, were first required to parade before His Majesty King George V at Buckingham Palace. The convoy of some twenty vehicles arrived in the Vosges region of France a few days later.

The Vosges region is in a mountainous area of France, running south from Strasbourg to Mulhouse overlooking the River Rhine and the Black Forest. The roads were far from ideal at the best of times. The Vosges descend abruptly to the plain on the eastern side, though on the Western, or French side, the slopes were less severe.

The first winter of the war saw the mountain passes blocked with snow and ice, and as winter gave way to spring, and spring passed into summer, the fighting around the area carried on without any let up. Section 3 continued to bring the many wounded down the steep zig-zag roads, the corners of which were under direct fire from the German artillery and sniper fire. During one particular engagement the ambulances operated for 18 consecutive days and nights without rest, on roads which were broken up by the incessant traffic and heavy shell fire, and which became a quagmire when heavy rain turned the dust into mud. Back axles would break, and vehicles would have to be towed home, but repairs would be made and they were returned to service as quickly as they possibly could.

In an article published in the *Austin Advocate Magazine* dated June 1916, Oscar Thompson gave a rare insight into his personal thoughts, and of the work on which he was engaged, when he wrote: "When this war ends – there may, as some people think, be an entire change in social conditions throughout the world. On the other hand, things may go on very much as before it began, but in either case it is safe to prophesy that relationships have been established between England and France which ensure a close and binding friendship for many years to come. It is strange how quickly the human animal merges itself into its environment. Here we are, all Englishmen, most of us speaking but little French, yet in a few months the local outstrips the general interest and a small skirmish in a vicinity excites the attention far more than a big battle at, let us say, Ypres. What splendid chaps these French soldiers are; the whole world knows what they have done, but to us ambulance workers who met them

Oscar Thompson with his driver Thomas Holdstock in Vosges.

41

A collage of pictures showing Austin ambulances in snowbound Vosges during the first winter of the War.

AUSTIN AMBULANCES IN THE VOSGES.

chiefly in their hours of sorrow, their fortitude, endurance, courage and optimism are a never-ending source of admiration and wonder. If only some of those curious creatures, who sit at home in comfort and shake their heads over our prospects of emerging successful from the great war, would acquire some of the confidence shown by the soldiers engaged in the task of winning it, what a lot of foolish talk we should be spared." Oscar continues ... "It will interest you Mr Editor, to know that Section 3 of the British Ambulance Committee contains no less than six Austins in its compliment of twenty. Three of these are the new 25hp models, two 18/24s and one, my old car 'Pobble,' a 40hp. One of these cars, an 18/24 has seen fifteen months hard service, during which it has acquitted itself most admirably. 'Pobble' has done nine months' hard service and others, though comparatively recent arrivals have shown every prospect of successful careers. The section expects shortly, if the Austin Motor Company does not fall behind in deliveries, an addition of four or five new 25hp machines, which will make us largely an Austin convoy."

In praise of the Austin 'product,' Oscar continued thus: "Everybody has different ideas upon ambulance design, but the new 25hp Austin appears a very suitable and practical model. The suspension is excellent, and that, with an ambulance, is half the battle. Of our work here it is not permissible to speak, besides everybody knows what ambulances do up at the front: they advance in fear and trepidation as quietly and swiftly as they can; embark the wounded and bolt for all they are worth, and make holes in suitable places to show how they have been pursued by shells, shrapnel, etc, and take care not to give each other away. 'Pobble' has been hit three times, fortunately without damage to anybody, but perhaps after the preceding sentence the statement will not appear convincing. I enclose a photo of 'Pobble' and my chauffeur, Thomas Holdstock, who has just been awarded the Croix de Guerre for courage and devotion under shell fire."

Muriel Thompson had brought her own car over to France, which we understand to have been a Cadillac. This she named 'Kangaroo,' and referred to it many times in her war diaries. All the other vehicles in her section were also similarly named; 'Flossie' the Ford and 'Unity' the Unic ambulance, to name but two.

In an entry dated April 17th, 1915, Muriel states "Flossie's carburettor flooded after lunch, I hit it with a spanner and it revived. Parcels arrived from England – joy! A cake from Buzzard, also a lovely oil pump and pliers, just what I wanted."

Muriel must have thought much about those heady days not that long since she raced Pobble around Brooklands, for in her entry for September 7th, 1915, after leaving Lamark to establish a holding camp in the Loire, she wrote; "Up at 6.30 am and cleaned the car from 7 till 8. Found our coffee laid in a room with three British Officers. They talked to us and were very interested. Went to Belgian Etat Major who at once gave me a 'bon pour' (coupon) for 50 litres of petrol. Rouen looked lovely – we did so regret having to go without seeing it. Kangaroo ran beautifully. Stopped at Louviers and took snapshots of the car outside the catherdral. We lunched by the roadside in a wonderful empty world, and lay on our backs beneath a haystack, with blazing sun, and miles and miles of empty country, blue sky and not a human being. Lovely drive, but got very tired – mile after mile. Passed Évreux, Dreux, Chartres, Vendôme and reached Tours at dusk. The screen of the car broke, and it took us about half an hour to unship it. For miles the road lay as straight as a ruler, and quite empty, and I sighed for Pobble in his streamline days. Got to Azay in the dark and arrived at 8pm. Did 178 miles."

Obtaining spares for the variety of vehicles being used as ambulances was always going to be difficult, and in consequence had to be obtained as and when the opportunity arose. On one such occasion they came across a wrecked ambulance where the driver and the entire cab had been blown away, leaving the four stretcher cases unharmed in the back. As they were removed to another vehicle, the girls noted that the spare wheel remained undamaged – they now had two spare wheels for their ambulance. When, later, they were decorated in the field, they were told that the citation was really for the theft of the spare wheel.

Muriel Thompson was later awarded the Croix de Guerre along with several other fellow drivers, but as so many awards were recommended (sixteen Military Medals and three Croix de Guerre), their validity was questioned. However all the awards were supported by both French and British officers, and allowed, as each recipient had shown courage and coolness under fire. As one of Muriel Thompson's fellow drivers recorded after the war. "There is no glamour in starting up engines, but the girls said I should have been awarded a mangle handle rampant."

Oscar, though not physically wounded during the conflict, suffered what is today known as a mental breakdown. When he was fit enough to return to duties, he was sent to Paris by the Admiralty to act as a liaison officer with the French authorities on naval matters. After the war, he resumed his position as Chairman of George Thompson & Co, taking an active interest in shipping to and from Australia. This interest led him to study migration to this continent, and in 1929 – at the behest of the Government – he became one of the shipping representatives on the Overseas Settlement Committee, later to become a member of the Council of the Chamber of Shipping.

Oscar never took any further part

A very grainy photograph showing 'Pobble' on the right and another Austin named 'Quangle.' Originally published in the 1916 *Austin Advocate Magazine.*

Muriel Thompson (on the left) loading a stretcher into 'Flossie' the Model 'T' Ford ambulance in 1915.

in motor racing, preferring instead to channel his interest in playing golf, being a founder member of Sunningdale Golf Club. He never married, and died after a short illness from encephalitis lethargica (inflammation of the brain) on 20th August 1937, whilst in his 60th year.

Muriel continued her work with the FANY, and was to be mentioned in despatches, in addition to her other awards, she was also awarded the Military medal, decorated in the field by GOC Second Army, General Sir Herbert Plumer. By 1918, Muriel was the Officer in Charge of a mixed FANY/VAD. (Voluntary Aid Detachment) convoy working up by the front line at St Omer. Her diaries make many nostalgic references to Pobble, and also indicate that she even found time to visit her brother in Paris. Like Oscar, Muriel also suffered a breakdown brought on by exhaustion, and returned to England for recuperation. When her health returned she channelled her energies into becoming a recruiting officer for the Women's Royal Air Force, until she was demobilised on 1st October 1919.

After the war, Muriel remained with the FANY until 1922 when, following a difference of opinion she resigned. Like Oscar, she never married, and also died of encephalitis lethargic on 3rd March 1939.

Of Pobble? We know that it survived the war, and was fitted with a landaulet body. In a statement in *The History of the Austin Motor Company*, published in 1925, it advises that: "After its racing career, Pobble was fitted with an ambulance body, then, after four years' ambulance duty in France, a landaulet body was refitted and 'life proceeded as formerly." Again, in another Austin booklet published to celebrate the company's 'coming of age' in 1926, it is stated that "Pobble (after the War) continued to do its work in a highly satisfactory manner."

Additionally, the late Bill Boddy wrote to say that there was an unconfirmed sighting of it in the 1930s "somewhere in the Manchester area."

The registration number V33 still exists on a vehicle up in Scotland, its owner having been quite unaware of the amazing history that lay behind it.

(Author's note: I am indebted to Sir Andrew Leggatt for kindly allowing me to borrow Oscar Thompson's scrap book, from which I have been able to piece together the fascinating history of this particular Austin motor car, and also Lynette Beardwood of the Female Auxilliary Nursing Yeomanry, for allowing me to include photographs and extracts from Muriel Thompson's diary.)

Chapter 5
Sir Herbert Austin and the McKenna Duties

In May of 1915, Britain's Liberal Prime Minister Herbert Asquith was forced into accepting a coalition government, which brought several members of the Conservative party into the cabinet. However the Liberals insisted that the Chancellor of the Exchequer must be a Liberal, a post which was taken by Reginald McKenna.*

Reginald McKenna.   Sir Herbert Austin.

With the continuing loss of merchant shipping brought about by enemy U-boats, McKenna, though a staunch advocate of 'free trade,' was able to persuade the Government to accept an emergency measure of taxation on the import of all luxury goods, which was to cover private motor vehicles, although not lorries as these were deemed necessary to assist in the war effort, but bizarrely also included such commodities as tea and cocoa. These emergency measures were called the McKenna

Duties, and added 33⅓% on all such goods, and were to remain in place until May 1956.

During the early 1920s the duties were relaxed briefly between August 1924 and June 1925, but then extended in the September of 1926 to cover commercial vehicles.

During his address to the Austin distributors and agents on October 13th 1925, Sir Herbert Austin made reference to the reintroduction to the McKenna Duties, and went so far as to suggest that they be levied on commercial vehicles too. Now whether this did actually play a part in its extension the following year we will probably never know. He also suggested that perhaps a fairer way to tax motor cars, which at that time was based on horsepower, would be to add it to the price of petrol – so now we know whose idea that was!

In 1929 there had been a General Election; Britain now had a Socialist Government, and the intention to repeal the McKenna Duties was voiced during speeches made by both the Prime Minister, Ramsay MacDonald and the Chancellor of the Exchequer, Philip Snowden, who suggested that Britain should once again be re-established as a 'free-trade' area. This did not sit well with Sir Herbert Austin who could foresee a flood of cheap motor cars coming into the country and undermining the trade in British-made motor vehicles, and suggested in a response to this disclosure that if the Government were to go ahead with this idea, it could possibly lead to the Austin Motor Company having to close down the works at Longbridge.

Ramsay MacDonald was quick to reply to Sir Herbert Austin's letter, which he described as "threatening and blackmailing," and went on to remind Sir Herbert that the Emergency Powers Act gave "drastic powers to a Government to deal with anybody who deliberately conspired to interfere with trade." A reference no doubt to Sir Herbert himself!

In a statement to the Press Association, Sir Herbert said: "I am not in any way disappointed; in fact, I am very much interested to see in the newspapers that both Mr MacDonald and Mr Snowden are assisting me in bringing to the notice of the electors the dangers which will accrue if the McKenna Duties and safeguarding measures now in existence are repealed. I therefore consider it my duty, as head of a big industrial company, to draw to the attention of the electors, especially my own workers, to this matter at the present moment, because it would be no use to warn the electors when the damage had been done after the next General Election. Then they would wish that they had voted differently.

"I am quite willing to leave it to the judgement of the electors, especially those who know me, as to whether the letter I wrote is a 'blackmailing' letter. It was certainly not written with that intention. Every expression I used in the letter was the result of very careful consideration, because I knew it would be attacked by those who were anxious to prevent the Conservative Party from taking up the reins of Government again and completing the task which they have so ably begun and carried through in the past four and a half years. It must seem rather strange to the electorate to read such expressions as those in Mr MacDonald's speech, particularly the statement that he will not yield to any capitalist intimidation. Happily, we are not living in a country where efforts of that kind would be of any avail at election time."

At the 1931 General Election, Britain was to have its first National Labour (or National) Government, and the McKenna Duties remained in place. It was not until after the Suez crisis in 1956, that the then Conservative Government actually abolished the Duties, 41 years after they were introduced.

There is of course a certain degree of irony about this, and in particular Sir Herbert Austin's concern over abolishing this tax, because as we all know, from that year onwards our manufacturers came under considerable pressure, which forced many long-established names in the motor industry to close down, but the threat was actually not to come from across the Atlantic as initially thought, but from the Far East, where cheap but good quality Japanese products were now being flooded into the country as fast as the ships could bring them over. However, it was not until 2005 that the gates at Longbridge finally closed on Sir Herbert Austin's Works.

* Reginald McKenna was born on 6th July 1863. He was elected in 1895 as MP for North Monmouthshire and served as a Liberal in Herbert Asquith's Government. He retired on the fall of Asquith in 1916, and died at the age of 80 on 6th September 1943.

Chapter 6

George Clarke: the pompous be-caned 'Silly Ass'

George Clarke introduced his stage act using an Austin Seven around the same time as Clarkson Rose and Norman Long were performing their now famous 'Austin Seven' song in 1928.

The act, which involved his blue and yellow Austin 7 'Chummy,' was created as a direct result of him witnessing the problems encountered by an owner of a new Austin Seven who was having difficulties mastering the Seven's fierce clutch whilst attempting to drive it in a traffic jam through London's West End.

Predictably what followed relied considerably on the fierceness of the clutch, but what is remarkable was that this comedian used a perfectly standard 1925 Austin Seven 'Chummy' with which to perform his act that involved

George Clarke.

some hair-raising driving 'on stage' often with a 'passenger' who was invited up from the audience.

His act was entitled 'The New Car,' and the scene was set in the back garden of a suburban house. George would race onto the stage from the wings and head straight for the footlights, then just as the audience, and the musicians in the orchestra pit thought the car was about to drive straight off the stage and into the first two rows of the auditorium, George would slam the gear lever into reverse, and with a squeal from the tyres the little car would shoot backwards, much to the delight and relief of those nearest to the front of the stage. He concluded his act by driving the car through a 'brick wall' which brought the house down – in a manner of speaking.

Another trick which he often performed was to start the car by pushing it across the stage, then as it motored towards the wings threatening to demolish the scenery George would leap in and bring it totally under his control.

Such was the popularity of his act, that in 1929 he was invited to appear with the car on the Royal Variety Performance in front of Her Majesty Queen Mary, whom, it was reported 'rocked with laughter.' The car used for that performance came from the Austin showrooms in Oxford Street, and went straight back afterwards. Whilst it was

**On stage at the Royal Variety Performance in front of their Majesties
King George V and Queen Mary.**

in all respects a 'standard' model, he did loosen the shock absorbers, and by slamming the gear lever straight from first to reverse, side-stepping his foot off the clutch and executing hand brake turns he was able to make it perform the most remarkable tricks.

George was invited to repeat his performance at the next Royal Variety Performance on 22nd May 1930, which was in aid of the Variety Artists Benevolent Fund, and to which Sir Herbert Austin presented the car following its performance on stage.

George Clarke was to perform in two more Royal Variety Performances at the London Palladium in front of His Majesty King George V and Queen Mary, but not always in the Austin.

In an interview in the summer of 1930 with Charles Vivian of *The Motor* magazine, Clarke said: "I do the most outrageous things; I suppose I ought to strip the gears at least once a week, but actually, I've never had any sort of trouble with the gearbox," – although he later admitted to breaking a half shaft or two.

However, Clarke's activities were not without incident, and in an interview with society journalist, Madeleine Grey, also in 1930, he said: "I drive very near to the footlights, and when I did my first 'turn' I used to drive backwards and forwards towards them. On one night in question I did this as usual, but by some mischance my foot slipped off the foot brake and jammed the accelerator down. I could just see out of the corner of my eye the car making straight for the footlights, and I was quite unable to get my foot off the pedal as it had become wedged. Fortunately I had the presence of mind to pull on the handbrake, and drew up within inches of the edge of the stage. It was the girl in the back of the car I felt most concerned about as I had visions of the car turning right over on top of her. I do not drive backwards down the stage now."

Clarke was extremely well travelled, and had worked extensively in Australia, New Zealand, Africa, and even Tasmania. He had also spent time in Paris, and played New York for no less than seven years.

In his interview with Charles Vivian he went on to say that the Americans dubbed the Seven 'the miracle car,' and it was once besieged at the Palace Theatre where it was on display front-of-house. "I received an SOS message imploring me to remove her as people were not only round her and in her, but were underneath as well." He then went on to say that he could have sold the car 'a hundred times over.'

The billboard advertising *Darling I Love You.*

He emphasised the car's standard specification by describing how, after one late show in New York he then drove the Austin 270 miles to Boston, to arrive on stage there before noon the next day.

Whilst Sir Herbert Austin may well have been pleased at the good publicity his Austin Seven was receiving in the United States, such exposure may well have been counter-productive, as with import duty it would attract a price ticket for $500, more than that of a Model 'A' Ford.

Although George made his name in London's West End theatres, and through

the medium of cinema films, he was never happier than when performing in the suburbs and provinces where he was billed as the pompous be-caned 'Silly Ass.' It was during one such performance that George encountered serious problems with the gearbox and needed to contact the local Austin agent to put it right. He was advised by the agent's manager that such repairs will probably take best part of a week, and offered him a brand new model from their showroom with which to do his act. To show his appreciation George presented the manager with two complimentary tickets for his next performance which were gratefully accepted.

George Clarke (inset) and a scene from the show.

However, on witnessing the way

'You can't park that here' – a further scene from the show.

in which this new motor car was being treated, the manager asked George to return it straight away, and advised him that his own car was now ready for collection!

By now of course, George and his antics with the Austin Seven had become so popular that a musical comedy, entitled *Darling, I love you* was written around them. The synopsis of the show revolves around a drummer and saxophonist – Bertie Bundy, (played by George) whose car-resistant wife – Bubbles, (played by Wyn Richmond), throws herself at any available man, an action which is only stopped when George shouts out "Darling, I love you." The band is invited to play for the Earl of Fawcett, at the mansion of Sir Herbert Sylvester, where a robbery takes place and valuable jewellery goes missing. Of course, there are plenty of opportunities for George to put his Austin Seven through its paces, as one would expect.

The show opened at London's Gaiety Theatre on 22nd January, 1930, and in spite of poor reviews ran for 147 performances.

In the March 1930 edition of *The Austin Magazine and Advocate* there appeared a full page advert for Mobiloil, no doubt keen to attach itself to the success of George's now famous car, and of course the musical written around it. Mobiloil lubricants were declared to be "the only oil officially recommended for all Austin cars!"

George died in hospital at Maidenhead, at the relatively young age of 60, on December 21st 1946.

Such was the success of George Clarke's performance on stage with his Austin Seven that Mobiloil decided to promote its lubricants on the strength of it.

You should see George Clarke drive his Austin Seven*!*

Where? Why in the successful musical play at the Gaiety Theatre, London
" Darling I Love You "

Mobiloil
REG? TRADE MARK

is there too because it is the *only* oil Officially Recommended for all Austin Cars

VACUUM OIL COMPANY, LTD. Caxton House, Westminster, London, S.W.1

Chapter 7

The 40 horsepower Austin 'motor home'

Harvey Du Cros was a major shareholder in the Austin Motor Company, with interests in Dunlop and Mercedes, amongst others, so it is not beyond reason that when his son, Arthur required a 'special' vehicle to be built, Sir Herbert Austin would have no hesitation in providing exactly what he had in mind.

The vehicle in question was what would be described today as a 'motor home,' a vehicle which could provide the owner with the comforts of home when touring at home or abroad.

Based on the 40 horsepower chassis, the finished vehicle, which weighed in the region of two and a half tons, and travelled at a comfortable 12mph was equipped with every conceivable luxury available at that time.

The length of the interior was 12ft 3in, whilst the roof, being built in the clerestory fashion allowed good head room and adequate ventilation.

The body was made from English ash, panelled in aluminium, whilst the interior was panelled with mahogany, and the ceiling with satin wood.

The 40hp Austin on the Austin Stand at the 1909 London Motor Show held at Olympia, West London.

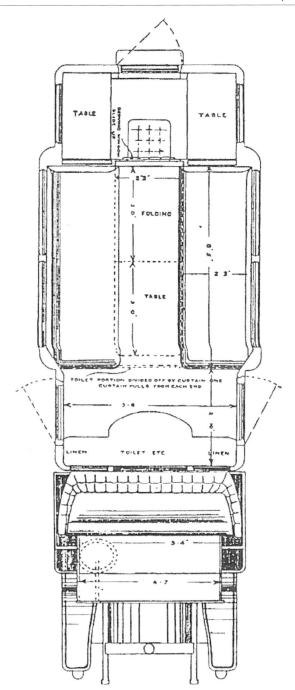

The vehicle was equipped with a toilet compartment containing a wash hand basin with running water, screened from the main saloon by a curtain, whilst all the windows were fitted with interior blinds.

There were electric lights in the ceiling of the lounge, with a table lamp for reading, and another over the wash hand basin in the toilet, all run off the vehicle's battery.

The kitchen, situated at the rear of the vehicle, was equipped with an alcohol burning stove, over which the ceiling was panelled in aluminium for easy cleaning. Under the stove was a metal-lined drawer with a plug that was used for the washing up. The water for this was supplied from one of two tanks fitted in the roof, to which access was gained via the driver's compartment.

A folding four-person seat was carried in the front part of the roof, along with the spare tyres.

There was also a telephone installed to allow communication between the occupants and the driver.

Though designed to carry, feed and sleep four persons, the dining room was able to accommodate up to six persons in comfort.

The servants (the chauffeur and the chef) would

Plan view showing the 40hp Austin's accommodation.

Looking towards the rear of the vehicle.

Looking towards the front of the vehicle.

have to sleep in bunks stored on top of the vehicle which unfolded from what appeared to be a traveller's trunk, with a canvas canopy supported by two steel poles being the only shelter afforded.

Such was its standing, that the finished vehicle was exhibited on the Austin stand in the Great Hall of the Motor Exhibition held at Olympia in 1909, and where it was described in *The Automobile Journal* of 20th November as "The largest private car in the world."

No record exists as to whether the vehicle attracted any further orders, or whether this was the one and only Austin 'motor home' ever to be built.

What eventually happened to the vehicle is not recorded, but with the Great War just a few years away, it is more than likely that it saw service as an ambulance during that period. Arthur Du Cros, sent two fully equipped ambulance teams to France, paid for out of his own pocket.

Encamped in France during the French Grand Prix of 1912.

The roof affording an excellent view of the race.

Chapter 8

Murder at the Village

The onset of the First World War saw the Austin Motor Company change its production from motor cars to that of armoured cars, lorries, aeroplanes, aero engines, shells, guns, ammunition, and many other items with which to help the War effort.

Because of this, the number of staff at Longbridge was increased considerably, attracting skilled workers from all over the West Midlands. In 1912, the workforce numbered just 1800, but by 1917 that had increased to 22,000.

To ensure that his workforce was able to reach the Works on time each day, Herbert Austin decided to build a village close by in which to accommodate them. Land was purchased in Turves Green for £7750, and he arranged for cedarwood bungalows to be brought in from the Aladdin Company, based at Bay City, Michigan, USA.

The estate consisted of 200 red cedar bungalows and 25 brick-built semi-detached houses, which were interspersed at intervals to act as fire breaks.

Probably one of the first births to be recorded in the village was that of Joyce Dixon, who was born there in 1917. It was here that she grew up, and also where she was to die.

On leaving school, Joyce naturally sought employment across the road at the Austin Motor Company, where she became a typist in the massive typing pool.

Not a great amount is known about her early life, but at some time during her employment there she became friendly with Harold Oswald Merry, a sheet metal inspector from Redditch. They saw quite a lot of each other and inevitably formed a serious relationship. However, there was one slight problem, in that Harold was already married and the father of five children.

On March 29th 1942, the affair came to a sudden and violent end when 25 year old Joyce was murdered by strangulation, and her body dumped in a pond at the back of the estate, which was no more than three hundred yards from where she had lived, and where it was to remain undiscovered for exactly four months.

Suspicion immediately fell upon 40 year old Harold Merry who was duly arrested and charged with her murder, a charge to which he pleaded "Not Guilty."

However, investigating the murder, Detective Inspector Brown discovered that diaries kept by Joyce revealed that realising the futility of their affair, they had decided to end it all together by taking their own lives.

When Harold was confronted with this information he changed his plea to "Guilty" and confessed to strangling Joyce with his neck tie and putting her body in the pond at the back of the estate. He then went on to tell the court that it was his intention to drown himself, but that the water in the pond was too shallow, and therefore could not do so.

At that time the only water nearest to the estate was the moat around the old Hawksley Farm, which was near to Longbridge Lane, but the water here was considered to be very deep and of more than a sufficient depth for Harold to have drowned himself there, had he a mind to do so.

Harold Oswald Merry was convicted of the murder of Joyce Dixon and sentenced to death by hanging. An appeal against the sentence was rejected, and on Thursday 10th September 1942 he was hanged at Winson Green Prison, just 165 days after committing the crime.

The hangman was Albert Pierrepoint, who was known as 'The Hanging Man,' and when he was not engaged in carrying out these official duties ran a pub called the 'Help The Poor Struggler' at Hollinwood, near Manchester.

Chapter 9

Testing the 'new' Austin 12/4

Although the Austin 12/4 first appeared whilst the Austin Motor Company was in the hands of the receiver, back in the autumn of 1921, it was not until the early months of 1922 when it was offered to a very keen and receptive market of owner-drivers. An account of how these cars were tested was published in the June/July (1922) edition of the *Austin Advocate Magazine*, several months after its launch. Although the author of the following piece is identified only as 'LAB,' which one assumes were the writer's initials, it deserves to be reproduced in full for our enjoyment, even though it was written almost a century ago.

TESTING THE 'TWELVE' – ASSURANCE DOUBLY ASSURED
I shall never be content now until I possess an Austin car of my own. Recently I watched and took part in the tests of an 'Austin Twelve,' and I am satisfied – more than satisfied. For a long while I have written praise of the 'Twelve' because I believed it, but now I know. I had ridden in one on several occasions previously, but only quietly touring, doing, in fact, what any other car could do. On test, however, we performed feats that I verily believe no other car dare even attempt.

But I am beginning my story with the last chapter. The first test takes place in the engine test house. Here the assembled engine is connected to a hydraulic dynamometer that registers the brake horse-power developed at various engine speeds. The tester allows the engine to run for about half-an-hour and then makes any adjustments that are necessary. These are remarkably few and far between. All that had to be done to the engine I observed under test, was to fit a new set of piston rings and slightly adjust the tappet clearance. I afterwards saw the same engine mounted in a chassis and was told that it would now have to undergo a continuous running test. As I was already convinced of the capabilities of the engine, I did not wait for this.

(Author's note: the writer makes light of the fact that a new set of piston rings were needed, but this would have involved a complete engine strip down!)

SHAKING HER UP
Next morning I returned to the testing shop in time to find the chassis equipped in readiness for its road test, and mounted to the flimsy seat beside the driver with many qualms as to my safety in the immediate future. He depressed the clutch pedal,

Just a box for a seat, the driver, complete with trilby hat, puts the Austin Twelve chassis through its paces. (Courtesy *The Austin Advocate Magazine*)

slipped her into reverse, and we backed gently out through the narrow gateway. I was folding my arms complacently, pleased to find that testing a car was so comfortable after all, when a sudden sickening lurch forward caused me to grab the seat with one hand and my hat with the other, or I should assuredly have parted company with both. Another lurch, that nearly threw me right off, and we were careering wildly along the road at 50mph, with the wind roaring in our ears and every nerve and instinct keyed up to respond to the magic touch of speed. The absence of a windscreen, of course, considerably enhanced this effect. After a few miles of this, the driver slowed down and turned into a narrow lane with a terribly rough surface. "This will find out any loose bolts," he remarked as he again opened out, and the needle trembled over 35. There it stayed, too, while we bumped merrily along, this poor scribe trying hard to register sensations, but finding his whole time occupied in clinging on to the treacherous-looking soap-box-like seat.

OVER THE TOP – AT 30MPH

A lengthy stop, while the driver went carefully all around the chassis looking for faults – without success, then we were off again and headed for the test hill and home. This part of the test really seemed superfluous to me. The hill is a very stiff one indeed, but we flew over the crest in top gear without a falter, and the engine running as smoothly and quietly as if we were touring gently along on the level.

There was no sensation of climbing at all; it was as if the road were horizontal, but some absurd person had built all the houses at a sharp angle, and so home.

Concerning this day's test, one thing stands out indisputable. I had gone out with the feeling that testing a stripped chassis on the road was a thing of tradition, surrounded with a soft haze of the glamour of romance. Romance there certainly is, but the test consists, first and foremost, of material realities. The driver's one idea is to put a tremendous strain on every part of the chassis, so that not the tiniest defect can escape unnoticed. And very thoroughly and conscientiously does he carry this out.

Two days later the body was completed, and I was invited to observe the final, the 'finished car' test. And in truth it was a test. Such a drive I had never pictured in the most tangential exuberances of imagination. We seemed to get right away from

The engine receives
minor attention to
the tappet clearances.
(Courtesy *The Austin
Advocate Magazine*)

civilisation in a wild, wonderful country of ghastly roads and impossible hills, where road construction was a necessity but road destruction a habit.

A NIGHTMARE RIDE
We sped along a lane 4 feet 6 inches wide at an average speed of 40mph. The road was marked over its entire surface of loose stones with pot-holes, some of which were a yard across and 18 inches deep. While to complete the picture there was the most perfect pair of cart ruts I have ever seen, quite a foot deep. We were walled in on either side by steep clay banks, so that the slightest deviation from the track would have meant that this account would probably never have been written. And then the hills! One that we climbed had the amazing gradient of 1 in 3 for its last 30 yards. To climb it was like leaping at the edge of the world. Nor must I forget a word of praise for the driver. His skill seemed to be nothing short of supernatural. He knew to a quarter of an inch where he wanted the car to be, and he got it there every time. In one place the lane was too narrow for the car to pass, so we went through with two wheels up the perpendicular bank, he, nonchalantly driving with one hand.

THE RIGHT CONCLUSION
In time we returned to the Works. I had seen all the tests of the 'Austin Twelve.' And henceforth I am an ardent admirer of its qualities. That a car of medium power and price should combine comfort, speed and hill-climbing capabilities in such generous measure is a real tribute to Austin methods and ideas. I can only hope that some day I, who am poor and therefore sound my aitches, shall join the ranks of satisfied 'Austin Twelve' owners.

LAB

(Author's note: Perhaps I am being a little cynical, but I found some of the road surface descriptions just a little far-fetched for my liking, even given the poor state of our roads in Kent – a pot hole a yard wide by 18 inches deep – yes, well!)

Chapter 10

The Austin Unity Song

A company's success can depend, not only on the quality of its products but to a great extent on how those products are marketed.

There is no question that the range of motor vehicles manufactured by the Austin Motor Company in the latter years of the 1920s would certainly appeal to a very wide range of motorists. From the diminutive little Seven right up to the luxurious Twenty horsepower models, much favoured by the gentry and the carriage trade. The quality and dependability of Austin motor vehicles were second to none, and in many respects far outshone those of other manufacturers offering a similar range of vehicles.

As the 1920s came to a close, however, Britain was experiencing a tightening of belts, due to what we now know as the 'Depression,' and no matter how hard the Austin agents and dealers tried to sell their motor cars, with the country in the economic doldrums they were certainly not finding it easy.

In previous years, by way of thanking the agents and dealers for all their hard work, the Company invited representatives from the dealerships, together with selected representatives from the press, to attend a banquet at the Connaught Rooms, in Kingsway, London. For 1928, as in previous years, the banquet took place during the annual London Motor Show, held at Olympia between 11th and 25th October.

The Austin banquets were lavish affairs, where good food and fine wines were always to be expected, and therefore greatly looked forward to, if only for the generous 'gifts' which they received for their loyalty to the Company.

As an example of just how lavish these events were, we jump ahead a couple of years to 1930, when it was held on Monday 20th October. Again, during that year's 'Motor Show'. The 770 invited guests were offered a choice of Huitres de Whitstable, or Hors d'Oeuvres, Torture Verte au Madère, Filets de Sole au Vin Blanc, Poularde Edward VII, Neige au Curaco, Mignonnettes D'Agneau, Fleuriste Pommes au Beurre, Perdreau en Cocotte Chez Soi Salade Panachée, Mousse Glacée, Petits Fours et Café, whilst the wine list included 1888 Choice Old Cognac, 1921 Charles Heidseick, and 1919 Moet & Chandon Champagnes, not to mention Barsac, and 1924 Chateau Pontet Canet Claret. There were also cocktails, sherry, cigars and cigarettes freely available for the invited guests.

However, when the guests arrived to take their seats on the occasion of the

1928 banquet, they were intrigued to find a large brown paper envelope on the table in front of them, with strict instructions not to open them until told to do so. When they had finished their meal, instead of the usual 'pep' talk from Sir Herbert Austin KBE, they were surprised to see, through the medium of cinematography, the toasts, speeches, messages and responses thrown up onto a screen. This was followed by a film portraying various sporting and other events in which Austin cars had taken part. When the 'film show' ended the guests were then invited to open the sealed envelopes. Inside, they discovered a gramophone record and a printed copy of the words and music.

On the disc's yellow label was printed the following: His Master's Voice, New Mayfair Dance Orchestra, Austin Motor Company Ltd, Longbridge, Birmingham, and the title *The Austin Unity Song*. Recorded 7th September 1928, with reference number 2-04665. It also stated that the music was by Vivian Ellis, lyrics by Collie Knox and the vocals were by Eddie Gross-Bart.

At that point, the Connaught Rooms orchestra (Arthur Crudge's British Imperial Orchestra) struck up the opening bars, and the assembled guests were invited to sing along to the words printed on the enclosed music score, and also projected on the cinema screen, and thus "The Austin Unity Song" was played and sung in public for the very first time.

As can be imagined, the guests were not greatly impressed with that particular year's gift, and in spite of, or probably because of, the food and wine which had been

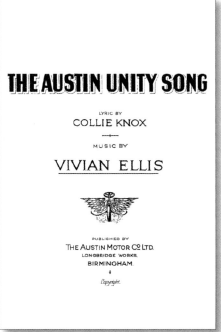

The front cover and title page of the *Unity Song* score and lyrics.

consumed, it is believed that very few of these records actually found their way home afterwards.

In the 1928 November edition of *The Austin Magazine & Advocate*, the 'event' was thus recorded: "Another distinct novelty was the 'community' singing of the "Austin Unity Song," which, went with a swing. On leaving the hall each guest took with him as a souvenir a copy of the song with music, and a record in jazz of the Austin Song."

Whilst *The Austin Unity Song* may not have been a 'hit' with the guests, it certainly went down well back at Longbridge, where it was often played over the Work's Tannoy system.

The lyrics of *The Austin Unity Song* were as follows:

Unity of purpose is our watchword every day,
In all we do and say,
Marching on our way,
Holding all before us as through life we go along, Hear the happy throng,
Sing the Austin Song.

Refrain:
We stand united
With Austin as our aim,
Our path is lighted with progress for the flame.
No shirkers, all workers, all playing the game,
For good will and fame.
Shoulder to shoulder,
Secure against the fall.
Bolder and bolder, we'll try to conquer all.
We'll fight for, do right for, the good of our name.
We stand united with Austin as our aim.

Loyal co-operation is the test of brotherhood,
Working as men should,
For the common good.
Each-for-all our motto,
As the race of life we run.
Striving all as one.
Through the years to come. *(Repeat refrain)*

The lyrics were by Collie Knox and the music was composed by Vivian Ellis.

Chapter 11

The Kensitas car

❝An Austin a day is given away" (except Sunday) was the heading printed on coupons found inside packets of 20 Kensitas cigarettes purchased during 1932.

The Austin in question was a brand new, 12 horsepower, six-cylinder 'Harley de-luxe' four-seater saloon car with a total value of £235. Described as a luxuriously modern car, with sunshine roof, selected hide upholstery, Triplex glass, bumpers (fenders) both front and rear, four wide doors, four wheel brakes, finger-light steering, a 13.9 six-cylinder engine, four speed twin-top gearbox, five wire wheels, and with all exterior bright parts chromium plated. And all you had to do to win one was to describe – in no more than 20 words – your opinion of the quality and merits of smoking Kensitas cigarettes.

Printed on the coupon were 'suggestions' as to the words which could be included with your answer, such as: 'Real Virginia,' 'Plus,' 'Naturally present in every tobacco leaf,' and 'Kind' – and, in order that they should not be missed, these words were also underlined.

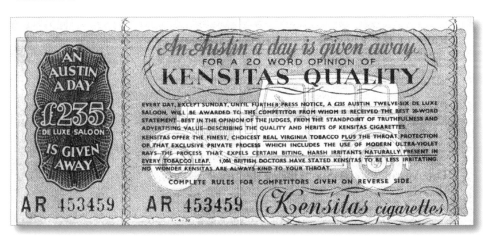

Front of coupon showing details of the competition. (Courtesy oldclassiccar.co.uk)

The reverse side of the coupon which contained the rules and entry form.

The competition commenced on 1st April, 1932, and on the front of the coupon was an explanation of what the competition was all about. The rules were to be found on the reverse, together with the 'tear-off' portion of the entry form upon which you inserted just two of the words which you considered best described the quality and merits of Kensitas cigarettes. It can be seen that in order to enter this competition you first had to purchase, and therefore 'smoke' the contents of 10 packets of cigarettes.

The first two words placed on the tear-off portion were then to be marked as number 'one' and number 'two', with the subsequent words of your statement added on the next nine portions, to be marked accordingly '3' and '4', and so on, until all ten portions had been completed with twenty individually numbered words in total.

Of course, what they did not tell you was that after purchasing ten packets of Kensitas and smoking 200 cigarettes, you may by now have put your health at some potential risk, even though, according to "Over 1000 British doctors, Kensitas cigarettes are less irritating," (than what? one may ask) "and are always kind to the throat." But then, we only know with hindsight that this was probably not a very sensible thing to do.

The advertising stunt was instigated by the Austin Motor Company's Public Relations Manager, who made 179 saloon cars available to J Wix, the owners of the Kensitas name, at a very cheap price, delivered, as required, to each winner direct from the factory. However, the MAA (Manufacturer's Agents Association), did not approve of the way in which the Austin Motor Company's manager had fixed the deal, and felt that the cars should have been sourced through their agents.

By October of 1932, the MAA eventually conceded that this method of selling was not against the interest of the dealers and agents, and peace was once again restored.

It would be most interesting to know just how many Austin 12/6s were actually given away during the life of this competition, however one latter-day Press & Publicity Manager did tell me that the campaign was not considered to be a great success and that he did not believe that very many Austin 12/6 'Harley de Luxe' saloons were actually won in this competition.

What we do know is that at least one 'prize' Austin has survived and has only had two owners from new; having initially been won by a Dr Ogg of Bishopsgate, Glasgow, and on this occasion it was not delivered direct from Longbridge but actually supplied through Carlaws Cars Ltd of Glasgow. A paragraph in the *Daily Mirror*, dated 14th June 1932, shows that up to that date, at least 120 cars had already been won, when it announced that Mr Richard East, a foreman sawyer, of 38, West Grove, Gypsyville, Hull, was the winner of the 121st Austin saloon motor car.

Further research has thrown up a few additional winners, and even some of the winning slogans. One winner, a Mr Smith, who was a radio engineer from Hazelmere, in Surrey (No 174 – 15th August 1932) came up with: "The revolutionary method of manufacture utilizing choice tobacco renders smoking Kensitas cigarettes a delight, and fully free from irritating effects." Winner No 176 – 18th August 1932, won with: "The non-irritant qualities of Kensitas cigarettes, together with their cool and mellow smoking, prove the value of scientific manufacture." And finally: a Mr Cookson from Leeds won his Austin 12/6 with: "The delightful fragrance which is predominant in Kensitas cigarettes is due to expert blending and exclusive scientific process of manufacture."

The Austin Twelve-Six 'Harley de Luxe' which would have cost £235 in 1932.
(Courtesy Ron Kentish)

Chapter 12

The ubiquitous Austin Seven

In 1922, the Austin Motor Company launched a small four-wheeled motor car onto the postwar market – a motor car which was to revolutionise the way the motoring public travelled – and almost, at a stroke, decimated the thriving motorcycle and sidecar industry. The little motor car was, of course, the ubiquitous Austin Seven, which proved to be so successful that it was later manufactured under licence in other parts of the world, and was the precursor of such companies as BMW, Nissan, Jaguar, and Jeep.

It was on a return journey to their home, Lickey Grange, one very wet and rather unpleasant evening that Sir Herbert Austin's wife, Helen, noticing the discomfort suffered by families travelling on motorcycle combinations, turned to her husband and suggested that with his brains, he should be able to develop a motor car which would cost the same as a motorcycle combination, but provide the occupants with a safe comfortable journey, whatever the weather. Sir Herbert, however, had other rather more important matters on his mind at that time, as his company was suffering a serious downturn in trade, and was already in the hands of the receivers.

Herbert Austin seated
in the Austin Seven
prototype.
(Courtesy R J Wyatt)

67

It is understood that the matter was later discussed with board members, who scoffed at the idea, as, after all, they had the superb Austin Twenty (which few people could afford), and the newly launched Austin Twelve-Four, which was yet to make an impact, and they could certainly not see the need for a miniature motor car as well. It was then that Sir Herbert took the decision to go it alone, even threatening to hand the idea over to Wolseley, a company of which he was still a Director, as he already had a few ideas as to how such a small motor car should look. The Austin Motor Company's chief cashier owned a very small motor car, an eight horse-power Rover, which had a two-cylinder, horizontally-opposed engine, and was proving to be a very successful little motor car, so why not produce something along much the same lines?

The Rover 8 was 'borrowed' from the chief cashier, examined and measured in considerable detail, and thus provided Herbert Austin with ideas as to how such a small car should eventually look.

Austin had been granted (no doubt with some reluctance) the sum of £1500 to produce three prototypes of this small motor car. The design aspects of this project were undertaken at Sir Herbert's home, Lickey Grange, and he even took one of the company's draughtsmen, 18-year-old Stanley Edge off the company payroll, installed him up at the Grange, and paid his wages out of his own pocket.

Over the next couple of months, various ideas were discussed, and either acted upon or discarded. Young Stanley was instrumental in getting Sir Herbert to ditch the two-cylinder engine idea in favour of a proper four-cylinder engine, developing just under seven horsepower, an engine which was, in effect, a scaled-down version of the four-cylinder Austin Twelve and, of course, the Twenty.

When the design work had been completed to Sir Herbert's satisfaction, the project was then moved down to the Works, where the three prototypes were to be built. However, he was not at all happy about certain employees, or, of course, the receivers, being aware of what he was up to, so he had the area in which the work was to take place screened off, to keep out any unwelcome visitors.

Once Austin was ready to start putting his ideas into practice, a few others were brought in from the Works to assist with the project, namely Alf Depper from 'Experimental,' a supervisor, two or three fitters and an apprentice.

The three prototypes were finally completed by Easter Saturday, 1922, and were considered to be ready for testing. Only one of the prototypes performed successfully, and an excited Herbert Austin was soon behind the wheel and drove off around the works to see just how well it performed.

Then, at around 6.30pm, with Alf Depper sitting next to him, he drove out of the Works, up the Lickey Road and on to the Grange to show it off to his wife, who, when asked what she thought of it, simply remarked that it needed cleaning, "Then come and clean it," was Austin's reply. After a quick check over, Austin drove it down to Wychbold, and then returned to the Works without encountering any problems.

The Austin Seven was launched at a reception for press and agents at London's Claridges Hotel on 21st July, 1922, and to say that there was serious concern and deep scepticism would be to put it mildly. One young man was even heard to say to Austin that the public would simply not accept such a motor car, to which he replied: "But I am educating the public." The young man was Billy Rootes, of the Rootes Group, who, at that time ran a very important and well respected Austin dealership. And educate

Herbert Austin's two daughters, Irene and Zeta. (Courtesy R J Wyatt)

Exactly how Herbert Austin's wife envisaged a small four-wheeled motor car should be used. (Courtesy R J Wyatt)

the public he did, for the Austin Seven became the most sought after small 'proper' motor car, and was to be manufactured under licence in France, Germany, Japan and even the United States of America, where it was called the Bantam. It spelt the end of the alternative 'cycle cars,' and also the need for families to travel in discomfort in motorcycle sidecars.

It was the Seven of course – along with the now popular Austin Twelve that took the Austin Motor Company out of the hands of the receivers, and helped restore the Company's fortunes once more.

Today there are still almost 12,000 of all the variations of the Austin Seven providing economical and enjoyable motoring all over the world. There are over 44 clubs in the UK, and 19 in other countries, which cater exclusively for the 'Seven,' and there are over 50 specialist companies geared up to manufacture and provide essential spares ensuring that the Austin Seven will still be around for many years to come.

Aimed at lady drivers – this young lady was thrilled to be given an Austin Seven 'Chummy' as a present.

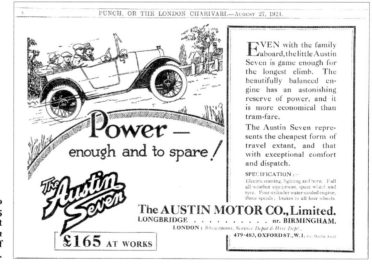

Power enough to spare at just £165 says this advert from the *London Charivari* of August 1924.

Chapter 13

'Time off' to go to the pantomime

Bobby Hewitt, the personal secretary to Herbert Austin, occasionally had apprentices in to help him with his day-to-day duties, working for a five-and-a-half-day week which always included Saturday mornings.

One such apprentice had made arrangements to visit the theatre to see a pantomime, and accordingly asked Mr Hewitt if it would be possible to have the time off on Saturday to attend.

Mr. Hewitt advised the lad to speak directly to the 'Old Man' on the matter and hopefully gain his permission.

On approaching Sir Herbert, the lad was asked what pantomime he intended seeing. "Ali Baba and the Forty Thieves, Sir", he replied. Whereupon, Sir Herbert led him over to his office window which overlooked the machine shop, and said: "Look down there lad, and you'll see all the thieves you want."

It is not recorded whether or not his request was granted.

Chapter 14
Vernon James Austin
(1893-1915)

Vernon J Austin.

Vernon James Austin was born on 21st November, 1893, the second child of Herbert and Helen Austin. Their first, a daughter named Irene, was born two years previously.

Vernon was a bright lad, and was educated at St Cuthbert's Boarding School, Malvern Links, in Worcestershire, before being sent down to Kent in September 1907, where he was to continue his education at The King's School, in Canterbury.

As was common with most public schools, The King's School was used as a stepping stone for those wishing to pursue a military career, and it was not long before Vernon enlisted for the school's Officer Training Corps. This led him on 6th January, 1912, to a commission in the Special Reserve of The Royal Artillery as a 2nd Lieutenant.

With his father being in the forefront of the motor industry, it was inevitable that Vernon would become interested in the motor cars manufactured by him at Longbridge, and he also had ambitions of becoming a racing driver, a pursuit at which he became most proficient.

Vernon had decided to enter a race organised by the Automobile Club of Russia, and was due to sail there when, just before he was due to embark, war was declared between Great Britain and Germany.

Now, holding the rank of Lieutenant, he was sent to Bulford Training Camp on Salisbury Plain, where he underwent further training as an officer. On 17th August, attached to the 22nd Battery of the 34th Brigade Royal Field Artillery, he arrived in

On horseback. (Courtesy King's School, Canterbury)

France to support the 2nd Infantry Division, where he saw action at the Marne, the Aisne and Ypres.

On the morning of 26th January, 1915, he, and his commanding officer, Lieutenant Colonel Sandilands (OKS – Old King's School), went forward alone to reconnoitre an area near La Bassée. On returning to his unit, he and Sandilands were forced to break cover and run along an open stretch of roadway. It was here that a German sniper had Vernon in his sights, and he was shot in the right side of his chest. He immediately lapsed into unconsciousness, and died within a few minutes of being shot.

In a letter to Vernon's parents, Lieutenant Colonel Sandilands wrote the following:

"Your son, who was a Subaltern in my battery, was killed in action this morning about 11.30am. The poor boy and I were alone when he was shot by a sniper. He had accompanied me to a forward position in order to learn the ground, never at any time a very safe business, but necessary. Coming back, we had to pass an exposed piece of road. It was at this point that he was shot through the right breast by a rifle bullet, and died within a few minutes without regaining consciousness. I need hardly tell you what a gloom it has cast over the officers and men of my battery, as everyone was so fond of him.

"He was such a cheery little chap and always showed such a stout front under fire. He was a keen and capable officer and he is a great loss to the brigade, with all of whom he was so popular."

The repatriation of the remains of those who fell in battle was not encouraged during this time, and in order to deter those wishing to do so, the War Office required the cost involved to be borne by their relatives, but Herbert Austin wanted Vernon's body to be brought home, whatever that might take, as he wished his son to be buried near his old school in Canterbury.

It is widely believed that in this respect he was aided by Harvey Du Cros, who made arrangements for the body to be transported home in one of the packing cases used to carry spare vehicle parts, namely, rear axles.

The body was brought over from France and arrived at Folkestone Harbour, where it was met by the undertakers, Messrs Hunt & Sons, who then brought it to Canterbury by motor hearse.

At 3pm on Saturday 6th February, the cortege arrived at Canterbury Cathedral, where the coffin was placed in the Holy Innocent's Chapel. It was met by the Rev Canon Mason and Dr McDowell, Headmaster of The Kings School, and also by a guard of honour composed of The King's School Officer Training Corps.

A short service was conducted by Canon Danks and the Rev A J Partridge, at which Herbert Austin and a few personal friends were present. The funeral then took place with full military honours on the Monday afternoon at St Martin's Church, a short distance away. Leaving Canterbury Cathedral, the funeral procession was headed by a firing party from the 3rd Cavalry Regiment stationed at Canterbury Barracks under 2nd Lieutenant Clifford, and was followed by the band of the 3rd Reserve Cavalry Regiment, through Burgate and Longport to the strains of the *Funeral March*. The coffin was borne on a Royal Horse Artillery Gun Carriage and was draped with the Union Jack, on which was placed Vernon's sword.

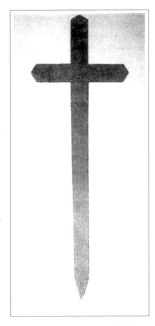

Vernon's father, Herbert Austin, followed the gun carriage as the chief mourner, and was accompanied by several friends and a large number of people who witnessed the committal rites, which concluded with the firing of three volleys over the grave and with cadets from the School's Officer Training Corps sounding of *The Last Post*.

At the service, the choir sang *Oft in anger, oft in woe*. There were two floral tributes from Father and Mother, two from Uncle Harry and Auntie Gladys, The staff at Lickey Grange, Directors of the Austin Motor Company, staff and workpeople of the Austin Motor Company, staff and boys of King's School, and many others, including one from the continent. Not the least touching object in the moving military ceremony was a plain wooden cross that was laid on the coffin with the sword, and bore the inscription in hurried handwriting: "A last adieu from his comrades on the battlefield" which had marked the spot where rested all that was mortal of a gallant lad who had died doing his duty to his country.

Vernon was just 21 when he was killed, and, had he survived, was destined to take his place at the head of the Austin Motor Company. We can only guess at what

The wooden cross which marked the spot where Vernon fell, and which now takes pride of place in the memorial chapel of his old school.

influence he may have had, or what changes he may have caused to its history.

We do know that Herbert Austin remained single-minded in his pursuit of excellence for the remainder of his life, which may, or may not, have been influenced by the tragic death of his only son.

The wooden cross bearing the message from his comrades occupies pride of place in the memorial chapel of The King's School, Canterbury. The plaque, which reads "This tablet was erected in memory of a brave soldier by the employees of The Austin Motor Company of Birmingham, London and Manchester" is mounted just inside the entrance to St Martin's Church.

He is also commemorated at Moseley Rugby Club (since relocated), and on a war memorial just outside Lickey Church.

Plaque erected to Vernon's memory located in the 1st Century church of St Martins, where he is also buried.

Chapter 15

Touring around Australia by Austin 12/4 in 1926

PART 1: INTRODUCTION

Austin motor cars have never been afraid to take their owners on long, and sometimes hazardous journeys. We only have to look at the exploits of the late John Coleman who drove his little Austin Seven from Buenos Aires in Argentina right up to New York. Then, of course, there was Miss Gladys De Havilland, who drove her Austin Seven across the world to New Zealand. 'Mugwump,' the 1930 Austin 16/6 Burnham Saloon, driven by students from Bristol University all the way to Johannesburg in the early 1960s, and then driven back again by South African students. And, of course, not forgetting the numerous pensioned-off Austin 12/4 Taxicabs in the 1950s, again mostly driven by students, to all manner of unlikely destinations across the world – and, after clocking up many thousands of miles, plying for hire around the streets of London.

Back in the early 1920s there was a craze (if we can call it that) to drive a motor car around Australia – a distance of approximately 10,000 miles. When you consider what the roads must have been like at that time – if indeed there were any in some places – this too must rank amongst the craziest of trials of endurance for man and his motor car.

Several intrepid motorists set out to attempt this tour during the early 1920s, one such pair being a Mr and Mrs Jack Dorney, newly married, who completed their honeymoon tour in an Overland Whippet, and, being the first, set the stage for others to follow. In 1925 Messrs Woodward and Mayor completed the same journey, only to advise all and sundry on their return that they were all set to undertake the very same trip again.

Our story, however, concerns Wilfred (Fred) and Ellen Anderson who, after completing a tour of Southern Australia in 1925, decided to circumnavigate the entire continent in an anti-clockwise direction the following year, both journeys being undertaken in an Austin 12/4 motor car.

The *Sydney Morning Herald* reported:

"Mr & Mrs Wilfred Anderson, of Wagga, recently completed a motor trip round Australia. They left Wagga in an Austin car on August 31st for Sydney, and travelled thence to Brisbane, Roma, Longreach, Cloncurry and through the Northern Territory to Western Australia. After leaving Perth they visited Coolgardie, Balladonia and Eucla, traversed the desert to Fowler's Bay, and passing through Port Augusta, Mt Gambier and Melbourne, returned to Wagga. The car was fitted with collapsible beds, cooking utensils and a table. Mr Anderson said that the stories of hardships suffered by round-Australia tourists were considerably exaggerated. Mr Anderson left for Sydney this morning."

The tour, as reported above, started off from their home in Wagga Wagga in New South Wales on 31st August, 1926, but they actually commenced their journey on 22nd September, eventually arriving back three months later on 22nd December. Their journey took them into Queensland, across the Northern Territory, down into Western Australia, across South Australia and back into New South Wales, but our story is actually in two parts and commences with the 'trial' run across South Australia in 1925.

Wilfred Anderson and his wife Ellen decided to undertake the tour around Australia in 1926, in a Holden-bodied Austin 12/4 open tourer – which was described in a newspaper report as an 'Empire' model. The Andersons, the report went on to say, "were not young people like the Dorneys, having both reached middle age." "In 1925 they had motored from Wagga Wagga in New South Wales to Perth and back, a distance of around 4500 miles, and were so charmed by the nomadic life they endured that they were determined to make an even longer trip – right around Australia the following year, and considered that the Austin 12/4 was rugged enough to withstand any rough roads which they were likely to encounter."

Wilfred Anderson was no stranger to the care and maintenance of the motor car, as he ran a garage in his home town of Wagga Wagga, so it should be assumed that he knew exactly what his Austin was capable of, and able to fix any problems which might occur during the journey.

The garage, as can be seen from the photograph, sold mostly American motor cars, such as Hudson, Essex and Dodge, and it was the last of these that actually helped to pay for their tour, for not long before they were due to set off, Wilfred received a letter from America advising him that he had won a trip to the USA, as a reward for selling

The Anderson's Garage in Wagga Wagga.

an outstanding number of Dodge motor cars. Wilfred replied that he did not wish to travel over to America, as he had still much to see of his own country – Australia, and asked whether it would be possible to have the monetary value of the prize instead. The company agreed to his request and provided the financial means to undertake the tour. Perhaps they may not have been so keen to do so, had they known the intention was to use an Austin!

Unlike other motor cars which had attempted this tour, the Austin, which was described as a sturdy British-made four cylinder motor car, had not been strengthened in any way. The springs on the Anderson's Austin, for example, were 'as fitted' at the factory, and even the Smith's shock absorbers, were, we are told, standard too.

In their drive to Perth and back in 1925, the Austin gave absolutely no 'significant' trouble, and the springs, having been adequately tested on this trip were considered to be more than capable to cope with the worst road conditions which they may encounter on their round-Australia adventure. However, having said that, the Austin was all but written-off on the very last leg of their journey – but, through no fault of the car itself.

From a newspaper cutting, published prior to their round-Australia journey in 1926, the writer commented that: "Admirers of the British car will watch with interest the progress of this car, because it will be one of the severest ordeals to which a British car has been subjected in this country."

The report then went on to comment on the various preparations which had been made for this journey and the addition of home comforts with which to sustain them throughout their adventure: "Mr Anderson has exercised great ingenuity in preparing the car for the journey. It has a large petrol carrying capacity for the long stretches between fuel supply stations, a large water tank, camping-out body, and accommodation for the large amount of luggage necessary on such a trip. The luggage includes folding chairs and a table, a cooking stove, shotgun, tarpaulins for shelter, and digging implements in case of an accident. A 'pull-u-out' winch is fitted to the front cross-member as an added precaution against being stranded. On one running board is a cosy kennel, in which their mascot, a dog which answers to the name of 'Kerry' is comfortably housed."

The report also mentioned that Wilfred Anderson had been in touch with Jack Dorney who lived in Brisbane, and from whom he was able to gain a considerable amount of useful information about his forthcoming trip, not only on the road conditions, but also on the type of weather he was likely to encounter in the various regions through which they were about to travel. Especially in the dreary north-west, where he was advised to avoid the wet season between late November and December when heavy rains usually sweep across that region with many areas becoming severely flooded.

The 'anti-clockwise' route chosen for this adventure was to head West via Toowoomba to Roma, then head North to Blackall, Winton, Comooweal, Newcastle Waters, and Katherine onto to Darwin. From Darwin they would proceed via Derby and Broome, and then go across to Perth, and back to Wagga Wagga via Port Augusta, Adelaide and Melbourne.

Jack Dorney was able to secure the services of the Vacuum Oil Company to ensure that there was always a supply of oil and petrol at various points on the route for his trip. Wilfred was also fortunate in this respect, and was assured that supplies of Plume

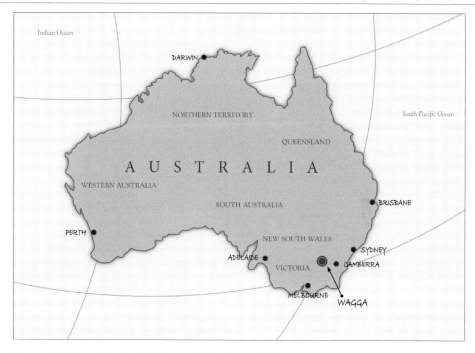

Motor Spirit and Mobiloil 'Gargoyle' oil would be available in readiness at various depots if and when required.

PART 2: 1925, THE FIRST TOUR OF SOUTHERN AUSTRALIA – PERTH AND BACK

The Andersons set out on their first, shorter 'clockwise' trip around the southern coast of Australia on Sunday 4th October 1925. Keeping them company, but driving a Buick, was Wilfred's brother Harry, his wife Florrie and their two children Freddie and Jean – who was known as 'Titch.'

The following is an account of that trip which has been reconstructed from the diary entries recorded by Wilfred's wife, Ellen, who had made meticulous notes of their journey, adding 'interesting' comments on the places they visited and the people whom they encountered en-route.

Florrie, Harry's wife, with their Buick Saloon car.

79

New South Wales & Victoria

The journey started off as planned, travelling during the day, stopping off to set camp for the night and to do a spot of fishing for their meals, which according to the amount caught, certainly in the early days of the tour, appeared to represent their basic diet for all meals including breakfast.

Their first encounter with poor weather conditions was at the Victorian border town of Orbost, where, during the night, the wind reached gale force and the rain was torrential. Ellen recorded Orbost as being a very beautiful area with many exotic birds – it was here that the Buick appeared to develop a very 'funny' squeak, but on investigation they found that the noise was coming, not from the car, but from the birds. With rain pouring down, they proceeded to a place called Marlo which was 10 miles off the main road, and running alongside the Snowy River for the entire 10 miles. Here the car slipped and slid all over the now saturated road, resulting at one point in the car turning a full circle and ending up an embankment facing the river, stopping just in time to prevent the car from sliding into it. Ellen recorded in her diary that she "became very frightened, the night was pitch black and it was raining like fury, I was very glad when the journey ended"

Wilfred and Harry, wearing oilskins, managed to erect the tents in the pouring rain, whilst the women and children kept dry by staying in their cars. Their comment regarding Marlo, was "there was nothing worth seeing there, it being a bit of a one-horse town."

They awoke the following morning to bright sunshine, and declared that now, "everything in the garden was lovely." After breaking camp they motored on to Tahmoor, on Lake Entrance, where they stopped for dinner. Here they walked down to the head of the lake, and waded through to the other side and across to Ninety Mile Beach – which was recorded as "a fine sight." However the lake was full of crabs, and Florrie, who waded across without shoes found that several crabs had attached themselves to her toes and nipped her badly.

After breaking camp, they headed off towards Melbourne, via Berwick, where they camped for the night. The next morning they drove into Melbourne and garaged the cars at a garage called 'Village Bell,' then took a taxi from there to the Victoria Coffee Palace, where they had a meal, and then went to see the play *No, No, Nanette* – which apparently they didn't think much of! After visiting Melbourne they continued on to Geelong, and camped 20 miles out, with the wind now blowing at gale force.

The following day they went on to Camperdown, and continued on to within a mile of Warnabool, where they camped near the beach for the night.

Ellen commented in her diary that "the country all the way is very pretty and all under cultivation, with no reserves of timber lying about since leaving Melbourne." It was at this time that Wilfred thought it would be funny to smoke a cigar, which unfortunately made him sick and feel very unwell. Ellen did little to help in this situation by singing *Freddy and his Wild Woodbine* (tobacco) – which was certainly not appreciated. They motored into Warnabool, then drove on to within 4 miles of Heywood. Here, Wilfred ground in a new valve to replace one which had burnt out, and also took the opportunity to repair the sun visor which had blown off in the wind. Rain was again causing minor problems, but the intrepid adventurers were quite relaxed about this aspect of the journey, as, by the time they reached Meningie, they now had a plague of mosquitoes to contend with.

Into South Australia

Saturday 24th October. After a night's sleep, they continued on to Wellington – which they considered to be "a one horse town," and where they had to cross the Murray River in a punt which cost them 2/8d for the fare. They were then able to continue onto Adelaide via Strathalbyn, which they thought to be "a very pretty little town". They spent that night camped out on Semaphore Beach at Port Adelaide.

When in Adelaide, they made enquiries regarding the road conditions out to the west, but no one whom they asked seemed to know anything about them, so they decided to drive onto Port Augusta and try there. At this point, Wilfred's brother Harry decided that he'd had enough, and so he and his family left Wilfred and Ellen to continue with their tour alone, and headed back to Melbourne, just 24 days into the trip.

Unfazed by Harry's desertion, Wilfred and Ellen pressed on, and after leaving Adelaide, drove just 5 miles into Gawler where they camped the night. The following day they headed off to Roseworthy, Farlee, Riverston and Auburn, where they observed that the harvest was in full swing. This led them into Watervale where they viewed an ancient church. From there they went on through Clare, Brinkworth and Krolunga which they noted was a great grape growing area.

On Friday 30th October they drove onto Warmertown, and on to Port Pirie, which turned out to be quite a fair-sized shipping town. They then continued on to Port Germein, which Ellen described as "a Godforsaken place." However, they did stop to do some fishing and were rewarded with three fish and a crab.

Another valve required grinding in before continuing to Port Augusta – described by Ellen as "a hot, dry, dismal hole of a place." Here they had to put the Austin on a punt which was towed by a small motor boat across the Gulf to Port Augusta West.

Still concerned about the condition of the roads, they went to the largest garage in the town, and also the police station, but could still not obtain any useful information. They also went to the railway station and spoke to the Station Master, who they understood had worked on the Transcontinental Railway since the line was first built, and he advised that because it was all desert, it would be quite impossible to find their way across it (even in an Austin Twelve). So, they decided to leave the Austin at Port Augusta West, and camped out in the Bush for the night, during which they endured a terrible storm that raged all through the night.

The Austin on a punt at Port Augusta.

Having weathered the storm, they decided to leave the car where it was, and took the Transcontinental train to Perth, which left at 9pm on Sunday 1st November.

In her diary, Ellen reported that "there was very little to see except plains, salt bush and sand" and recorded that "this was a dreadful country," however she also commented that the train was very nice to travel on. It was also noted that there were no railway stations along the line, so if you wanted to leave the train you had to climb

The Police Station at Augusta West.

down some steps in order to reach the ground. They broke their journey at Kalgoolie during the afternoon of 3rd November, and decided to have a look around. Here they did a spot of sightseeing, which took them to the Perseverance Mine where gold was first found in Australia by a man called Patrick Hannan.

On Sunday 8th November they took the tram into Neadlands, which was a pleasant ride along the Swan River, and in the evening went to hear the band play. Ellen recorded that she did not think the band was as good as the Wagga Band, and besides, she did not care for the selection of music they were playing.

The following day they did some sightseeing around Perth, and met up with a Mr Armstrong who had recently travelled from West to East across Australia. They were able to obtain a few tips from him regarding the road across the desert. He also described in some detail stories of the desert crossing, which so impressed the Andersons that they decided to return to Port Augusta for their car.

On Tuesday 10th November they left Perth in the Transcontinental train for Port Augusta, arriving three days later. The Austin, retrieved from the garage, was prepared for the long journey ahead and stocked up with supplies. On leaving Port Augusta they headed for Cowell, but decided to make a detour to miss the Yardee Sands which they had heard were 'very bad'. They continued onto Cleve and Rudat where they camped the night.

They commenced their journey on Sunday 15th November and promptly ran over three snakes, they also encountered a very large kangaroo whilst on the road to Lock, which they reported was very rough and sandy. The weather, it was recorded "was dreadfully hot." They arrived at Ellinstone at around 6pm, and drove on a further 20 miles where they set up camp.

The following day they continued on towards Streaky Bay, a very pretty bay, but a very poor town which depended on shipping and motor mail for its existence. From there they motored on to Murat Bay, which they reached at around 6pm amidst a very heavy thunderstorm. They parked up and remained in the car until the storm cleared, then drove on a further couple of miles to set up camp. It continued to rain on and off during the night, but the storm had cooled the air considerably.

Their next port of call was Thevenard, where fibro cement roads and Plaster of Paris was made. The Andersons recalled that the factory was very large, and had its own pier to accommodate the boats which transported their goods to Sydney. They also commented that they "were able to catch a nice lot of fish from the pier." (The jetty, built in 1920, was the first concrete jetty in South Australia).

Fowler's Bay, their next destination, was described none too flatteringly as another "one horse town," where the roads ended at the border of Western Australia, leading to only rough tracks from then onwards. However they continued their journey and went through Whitewells Station, which was described as a shanty of a place inhabited by a single white man, the others being local natives. They spent the night at Nullabor – a very lonely place on the plains.

Into Western Australia

The diary entry for Thursday 19th November reads: "Left Nullabor at 11.30. On the road we came across wombat burrows. Fred shot two of them; they are like bears to look at and are supposed to be good to eat. We had sport with two kangaroos, my word they can go some, beat us in the end. We passed two camel teams loaded with wool. We met a linesman doing his rounds, a very funny sight to see him travelling in a buggy and a pair of camels. From there we went on to Eucla where we camped for the night."

They had a quiet day at Eucla and went out on a turkey hunt, although they were not able to catch any, but they did manage to shoot a very large snake. They also played their phonograph to the Aborigines, and thought it very amusing to see their reactions which ranged from being 'concerned' to 'laughing' with amusement: "They thought it was a mystery boss." Ellen added further to their amusement by giving one gin (a name by which aborigine women were referred to) a hat and a coat – she was apparently so pleased with her gifts that she danced and sang in appreciation.

They left Eucla with some freshly baked bread, as they were unlikely to encounter any shops on the road where food could be purchased. They then continued on to Mundrabilla Station, which was owned by Mrs Ross Watson, a widow with three little children, who were the only white people in the place. After having lunch there, they left for Madura, which at that time was enjoying a long spell of very hot dry weather, their average rainfall being just 5 inches per year, an average which had not been reached for three years.

Madura Station consisted of a single hut which was occupied by Mr Gourdan the owner, all the other inhabitants being Aborigines, At Madura they had a very fine mineral bore, where the Andersons were able to have a hot bath and a swim. However

in getting out of the bath Ellen slipped on the slippery ground and broke one of her toes.

Before they left Madura for Balladonia, Mr Gourdan killed a beast for them so that they would have some fresh meat when back on the road, as the Stations were hundreds of miles apart.

On route to Balladonia the Andersons had to drive the Austin up a very rough gorge where they had to avoid

Ellen with Aborigines.

some very big boulders. There really was no road to speak of, and they discovered that the last car to go up the gorge had to be towed up with camels. The rough track and stones caused two of the tyres to puncture, which had to be repaired before they could continue. Thirty miles further on, Wilfred shot three fairly large wild turkeys.

By Monday 23rd November, the Andersons had reached Balladonia, after driving across country, through grass as high as the car, looking for tracks from car or horse, and getting lost into the bargain. But, with the aid of their compass, their route was finally worked out, and they arrived there safely. On the journey they met a linesman who was working over a hundred miles from home, in a place called Byre near Israelite Bay. They shared some of their fresh meat with him which was greatly appreciated, as supplies only arrived by boat every three months. Their arrival at Balladonia was aided by simply following the telegraph wires.

Balladonia was yet another 'Station' run by two bachelors: Mr Ponton and Mr Mason. All the other inhabitants were Aborigines.

From Balladonia they drove on to Cook's Station where they stayed the night, leaving the following day to Fraser Range where they encountered some very bad road surfaces. They stopped for lunch at the Range and then continued on to Norseman which they reached at 6pm – the first town for 900 miles, and were very pleased with their achievement.

The date is now Thursday 26th November, and after breaking camp they pressed on through enormous salt lakes, observing the amazing mirages on the Ary Lake. En-route they encountered two donkey teams, where they were amused to see a small donkey pulling such big wagons. There were 30 donkeys in one team and 25 in the other.

The roads were very bad from Norseman to Coolgardie, and when they arrived there they took the opportunity to post letters which they had collected from various people whom they had met on the road. Coolgardie, was at one time a very prosperous mining town, but had almost become derelict since mining operations had ceased. They continued for a further 15 miles where they camped for the night.

The Andersons continued their epic journey on towards Southern Cross – another mining town, where they were experimenting with wheat growing. Ellen commented in her diary that the crop they saw did not look up to much.

By Saturday 28th November they had arrived at the Slocum's place at Wild Catchem, where they were made very welcome, and stayed there until Tuesday 1st December.

They continued their journey back to Perth where they arrived at 6pm, and decided to garage the Austin for the night. The following day they went sightseeing around the beaches of Freemantle and Cottasloe, then around Perth itself.

A week later they loaded the Austin on board a boat bound for Melbourne, which took them seven days to reach. The Austin was offloaded after a pleasant trip, and they stayed the night with friends. They left Melbourne on Sunday 13th December at 10am, and reported that the roads to Seymour were particularly bad. They got to within two miles of Benalla when the steering arm broke, and the car went out of control. They dived off the road, over a large heap of stones, and headed straight for a tree, but by some miracle the stones must have bumped the wheel, and forced the car away from the tree and down into a culvert. Ellen recorded in her diary that she "took a firm grip and closed her eyes thinking that the end had come," but at that very moment they came to a standstill with the front wheels up a bank, and the rear wheels at the bottom of the culvert. "It was a wonder," she records, "that the car did not turn over." On examination, it was found that a rock had gone through the tyres, and that the chassis had been broken in half.

Undaunted, they decided to stop there for the night, and dig a trench in the morning to get the car out.

Being an Austin Twelve it was not surprising that, even after such a bad accident, the Andersons were still able to continue for a further 1½ miles to Benalla where they were able to find a garage which would carry out temporary repairs to enable them to get home.

They left Benalla on Tuesday morning after the repairs had been carried out, and by the afternoon they arrived home safe and sound. Ellen recorded in her diary: "All's well that ends well!"

And so ended the first tour which encompassed much of the coastal area of Southern Australia.

PART 3: 1926, THE SECOND TOUR – ANTICLOCKWISE AROUND THE ENTIRE CONTINENT

You would have thought that after such a trip, the Andersons had satisfied their sense of adventure, and were now prepared to settle down to a rather more sedentary life. But you would be quite wrong, as the following year they set off again for yet another tour of Australia in their Austin Twelve-Four, only this time taking an anticlockwise route around the whole of the continent.

Ellen's diary entries were less 'dramatic' on this occasion and there were gaps where nothing of any note was found to be worth recording, and regrettably very few photographs of places or people have survived.

Kerry in his
kennel.

Prepared and ready to go. John Lanaghan wishing the Andersons a safe
journey, Note: Kerry their dog in his kennel on the running board.

The Andersons departed from Wagga Wagga for Sydney on 31st August 1926. The Austin Twelve, a new one, was well equipped and provisioned for their long and arduous journey around Australia. They eventually left Sydney on Thursday 22nd September and headed North to Ravensworth after spending the night with a friend at Wiseman's Ferry. In the morning, they carried on to Tamworth where again they stopped for the night.

By the Tuesday they had arrived at Spicer's Gap, where they got held up on account of the rain, and apparently had had a difficult time in getting there. The rain continued for some considerable time, and they were held up in the mountains because of it. Ellen recorded in her diary that "the roads were deplorable, the soil was black and the tucker (food) getting low." Whilst holed up, they recorded that "a single-seater car came along and tried to get up the mountain, but in doing so it slipped down the side and into a hole."

By Friday they had not progressed any further, and were awaiting a team of bullocks, which eventually towed them, and other vehicles including a lorry, up the mountain. They arrived at Red Bank where, in spite of the torrential rain they were able to make camp there for the night.

Into Queensland

The following day they eventually broke camp and moved on towards Brisbane, where they arrived around lunchtime. They were disappointed to note that all the shops were closed, as it was half-day closing. They motored on to Glenna which was South of Brisbane and stayed with friends for dinner. In the afternoon there was a very heavy storm, which prevented them from leaving as planned, but as it was, they decided to leave there at midnight, even though it was still raining heavily.

By Monday 3rd October the weather had thankfully improved, and they were able to do some shopping and spend some time with the Dorneys, where they were able to gain some useful information on what they could expect on the next leg of their journey. They stayed for dinner, and later were shown the pictures taken by the Dorneys of their journey around Australia during their honeymoon.

By Wednesday, Ellen recorded that she "had done her washing and ironing and was feeling tired." The following day was spent doing some more shopping, getting things that were necessary for the trip, and stayed a further night with the Dorneys before setting off. On the Friday they were asked to pose for photographs for inclusion in the *Brisbane Daily Mail*, and were interviewed by the Editor, Mr Elkinson.

They left Brisbane at around noon on the Saturday, proceeding towards Ipswich, and were blessed with good roads. However, they had to take the road through Lowood, which Ellen recorded "was the most dreadful road she had ever travelled on." Eighteen miles out from Towoomba they pitched camp and spent the night.

After leaving Towoomba and arriving at Chinchilli, they took the wrong road, and had to return to Chinchilli after travelling 21 miles, and start again. This time, taking the correct route they eventually made it to Goombi which was, in their words, "a small railway siding," where they spent the night.

On Monday 10th October, they left for Roma and arrived there at 4pm. They had a good look round and met up with some friends. They were also able to load up with water and have a cup of tea. They later drove out to the bore, which had been lit up especially for the Andersons, and were told that the light from the bore could be seen some 12 to 14 miles away.

Ellen recorded very little over the next few days, other than leaving one place and arriving at another, until Sunday 16th October when they arrived at Cloncurry, and Fred needed to remove the gearbox, strip out the gears, and fix them. We are not told why this had to be done, or to what extent the gears needed fixing, but they stayed there until Monday in temperatures of 120 degrees of very dry heat, then obtained a few provisions and continued on to Devonport, where they had a parcel to deliver. Whilst at Devonport they visited the Molvern Hotel, and took time to inspect specimens of the minerals which had been excavated nearby.

The next port of call was Duchess, and then on to Dejarra, which Ellen described as "a town consisting of three tin shacks." Here they were able to refill the car with enough petrol to take them a further 900 miles. They pitched camp some 24 miles out of Dejarra, and it was here that Kerry, their dog, got loose during the night and was bitten by a snake. At first the Andersons could not understand why the dog appeared to be ill, and by the time they discovered the cause, it was too late to do anything to save him. Kerry died about 6am the following morning.

The loss of Kerry left a deep void in their lives and the Andersons were upset to the extent that they could not bring themselves to eat for the rest of the day. He was great company and they felt a great loss at his passing.

After experiencing some trouble with the starter motor they were able to press on towards Camooweal and Rankin where they camped for the night.

The Northern Territories

Their next stops were at Alexandria, Brunell Downs, and Anthony Lagoon, where they stayed the night with Mr McCann. Mr McCann was the local policeman, who, in order to make sure that they had fresh meat for their breakfast killed a goat for them. On leaving Anthony Lagoon they went on to Newcastle Waters where they camped for the night. Here, Ellen records there were hundreds of Aborigines – many of whom were naked!

On Sunday 23rd October they motored on to Daily Waters and camped at the No 3 bore. They noted that there were lots of camps there, due to the construction of the Darwin to Adelaide Railway line.

For the next few days their journey took them to Katherine, where the mosquitoes and caterpillars were troublesome. They were hoping to swim in the Katherine River, but decided against it when they were told there were crocodiles there. On the Thursday, Ellen noted that Fred was not feeling too well,

Ellen with aborigine children.

but they managed to get to the Victoria Station where they stayed the night and also managed to miss a very heavy storm.

After leaving Victoria, they motored on to Wave Hill, then Inverway, and on to Flora, where again there was a heavy storm raging, and torrential rain throughout the night. Ellen records that an inch of rain fell during the night, and that the Black Alvra River which they intended to cross the following day was in flood. However, they carefully attempted to make the crossing, and managed to reach the other side through sheer good luck. Ellen records that the water came over the running boards during the crossing.

The next few days only recorded the places where they stopped for the night - Halls Creek, Sousa Downs and Fitzroy Crossing, where they needed to be pulled across by local Aborigines, who would not come onto the burning hot sand until sundown, during which time the car became well and truly bogged down in the sand, and they had to spend the night at the police station.

The following day, after being extricated from the sand, they motored on to Livingard where they camped the night. By Sunday 6th November, they reached Yeda Crossing and once again got themselves bogged in the river bed sand of the Victoria River. They worked hard all day and night until 10.30pm to try and dig out the Austin, but were worn out as a result and even too tired to sleep.

The following day they managed to leave the river, and drove on to Broome, which they reached during the afternoon. Here they hoped to fill up with petrol but were unable to obtain any, as it needed to be sent across by boat. They stayed the night at the Star Hotel – still waiting for the petrol to arrive. As the boat transporting the petrol had still not arrived, they had to stay a further night at the hotel, and decided to use some of their spare time going to the cinema.

The boat finally arrived on Thursday 10th November, and they were able to fill up with petrol and continue on their way, camping at the telegraph station at Sagrange.

The next couple of days were largely uneventful, and they pressed on through Frazer Downs, Hammock Plains, Naligine, Wallal and on to Paldue, where they stayed the night with Mr and Mrs Thompson and Captain Mitchell.

On leaving Paldue, they travelled on to Marble Bar, Nulligine, and Ethel Creek (Newman), where Ellen records they obtained some birds!

On Saturday 19th November they reached Meekatharare, where they were able to

The Austin just about to leave Paldue.

collect their mail, and then carried on to Mount Magnet in the company of Mr and Mrs Martin, and stayed the night at a hotel.

By Tuesday 22nd November they had arrived at Norcia, and Ellen recorded that she was feeling very unwell. They arrived at Perth the following day, where a doctor was called to examine her. The doctor ordered her to go to hospital. Ellen spent the next seven days in the St John of God Hospital, but we are not told what was wrong with her. She eventually came out of hospital on Thursday 1st December. Here Mr and Mrs Martin left them, and boarded the Transcontinental train for Adelaide.

On Saturday 3rd December, Ellen went back to see the doctor to pay her bill and also to obtain a tonic, then left Perth for Kalgoolie which they reached on Tuesday 6th December, and then booked into the Railway Hotel until the following Sunday.

On leaving Kalgoolie they headed for Port Augusta, where they stayed for a couple of days, then packed up the Austin in readiness for their journey to Adelaide, which they reached on the afternoon of Thursday 15th December.

The last few entries in Ellen's diary were sparse, and probably reflected the fatigue which they both must have felt after making such an epic journey.

The final entries read thus:

Friday 16th "Got to [no place name given – probably Hamilton], camped the night, mosquitoes very bad."
Saturday 17th. "Left and got near Gelong."
Sunday 18th. "Got to Melbourne, stayed at the Entwistles for dinner, left in afternoon for Wagga."
Monday 19th. "Got to Mangoplah about 4 o'clock – Wagga 6.30."
Tuesday 20th. "Stayed in Wagga at Elsie's place."
Wednesday 21st. "Left for Sydney."
Thursday 22nd. "Got to Sydney."

And so ended a truly epic tour of Australia, in an Austin Twelve, travelling somewhere in the region of 10,000 miles in an anti-clockwise direction, over some of the most unforgiving terrain consisting of unmade roads, precipitous mountain tracks and flooded rivers. They encountered some of the most extreme driving and weather conditions known to man. The car, apart from the matter of the gearbox at Cloncurry, only required some minor repairs throughout the entire trip, which Fred was able to undertake at the roadside, but it came through with flying colours, proving that it was a truly dependable motor car. Why they did it? We shall probably never know. They were certainly not the first, and probably not the last to circumnavigate the continent of Australia.

Finally, an account of the Anderson's epic drive around Australia was recorded in the *Austin & Advocate Magazine* dated July 1928 – two years after the event took place.

(Author's note: I am indebted to Jennifer Hanson for allowing us to share her great-grandparent's amazing journeys, and for supplying the photographs and copies of Ellen's diaries in which she covered both tours, and from which this article has been drafted and illustrated.)

Chapter 16

Albert Ball (VC, DSO, MC) and the Austin-Ball biplane

Albert Ball was the son of Albert and Harriett Ball, and was born on 14th August 1896. His father, Albert Ball (senior), was an influential man of significant means, owning substantial property in Nottingham, who became a Justice of the Peace, an Alderman and Lord Mayor of Nottingham, as well as being on the board of directors of the Austin Motor Company, a position which he left in 1914, in order to concentrate on his political and civic career.

At the commencement of the First World War, Albert Ball (junior) decided to join the Sherwood Foresters, and was very quickly promoted to the rank of Sergeant, followed in October of the same year with him becoming a commissioned officer (Second Lieutenant).

In spite of his swift and well-deserved promotion within the Sherwood Foresters, and partly because he was assigned to training recruits, and therefore confined to these shores, he considered that perhaps he may be better suited as a flyer, where at least he could see some action.

Albert Ball (VC, DSO and MC).

In the following June he took a course of privately funded flying lessons at Hendon Aerodrome, and by that October had gained the Royal Aero Club's certificate, enabling him to request a transfer to the Royal Flying Corps where, after only a few months, gained his 'wings' as a pilot.

He soon became an accomplished flyer and was sent to France to serve with Number 13 Squadron, where he was to undertake reconnaissance missions. He was later transferred to Number 11 Squadron, a fighter unit, where he soon distinguished himself, and was awarded the Military Cross and two Distinguished Service Orders. By now he had earned the title of 'Flying Ace' and became something of a popular hero at home.

Even after leaving the Austin Motor Company, Albert Ball (senior) still had considerable influence there, and when Albert (junior) made it known that the fighter planes he was flying could be considerably improved, then the Company, which was heavily involved in the manufacture of fighter planes for the Royal Flying Corps, was more than happy to listen to what he had to say.

The outcome was the AFB1 (Austin-Ball Fighter Biplane No 1), which, whilst designed by C H Brooks, the Austin Motor Company's chief aircraft designer, included many refinements which had been suggested by Ball.

The aeroplane, which was referred to as the 'Austin-Ball Scout,' was a single-seat biplane of wooden construction with fabric covering. It weighed 1525lb (empty), or 2077lb (laden). It had a wingspan of 30ft, was 21ft 6in long, and was powered by a 200hp Hispano-Suiza eight-cylinder liquid-cooled engine. It was to be armed with a single 0·303in (7.7mm) Lewis Gun which was capable of firing through the hollow airscrew shaft. There was also to have been a similar weapon on a Foster mounting positioned on the centre section of the upper wing, designed to fire upwards, missing the tips of the propeller blades.

The AFB1 was designed to have a maximum speed of 138mph at sea level, and 120mph at 15,000ft, with a maximum ceiling of 22,000ft.

The time taken to climb 10,000ft was given as 8 minutes 55 seconds, and it was capable of remaining airborne for two and a quarter hours on a full tank of petrol.

Although permission had been given to build two prototypes, only one was ever constructed, and was allocated the serial number B9909. Trials at Martlesham Heath were very successful, with excellent handling and with better climb than the SE5a, which was in production at Longbridge at that time. However, by the end of October the testers at Martlesham Heath were instructed to remove the engine, and ship it off to Ascot, where no doubt it was to be installed into the airframe of an SE5a.

There is no record of what happened to the remains of the AFB1, which was probably just broken up, as the war was now coming to a close, and there was little point in introducing a new aeroplane at this stage.

Sadly, Albert Ball was never to see his aeroplane in flight, for on May 7th 1917, he and 10 other flyers from No 56 squadron, were engaged with German fighters over Annœullin, which lay behind the enemy lines.

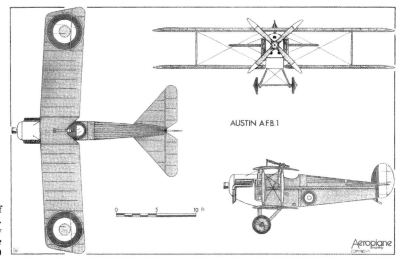

Diagram of the AFB1. (Courtesy *Aeroplane* magazine)

AUSTIN A.F.B.1

Three quarter front view of the AFB1. (Courtesy *The Austin Advocate Magazine*)

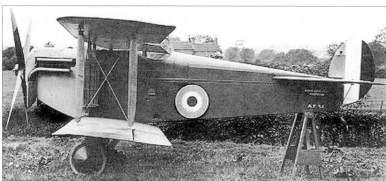

Side view of the AFB1. (Courtesy *The Austin Advocate Magazine*)

How Captain Ball lost his life still remains something of a mystery, as when his body was recovered from his SE5 biplane neither he, nor the fabric of the aeroplane showed any signs of damage caused by enemy gunfire.

An eyewitness said that after engaging with an Albatross D11 biplane, Albert flew into a very dense thundercloud. When he emerged, his SE5 biplane was seen to be flying upside down with a dead propeller; shortly after that, he was seen to lose altitude which ended in his crash.

His death was attributed to Lothar Von Richthofen (brother of 'The Red Baron') – though he had actually claimed to have shot down a Sopwith Triplane, not an SE5.

Ball was buried on 9th May with full military honours by the Germans, and mounted on the cross above his grave were the words: "In Luftkampf gefallen für sein Vaterland, Engl Flieger Hauptmann Albert Ball, Royal Flying Corps" (Fallen in air combat for his Fatherland, English pilot Captain Albert Ball).

Albert Ball (senior) purchased the field onto which his son crashed, and erected a memorial to him at the spot where he was found. The memorial is still tended by the children from the village school.

Chapter 17

The wedge and the office door

Bill Manning was born in Worcestershire in 1925, and lived his early life in Stoke Prior, which is just south of Bromsgrove, on the far side of the Lickey Hills, ten miles away from The Austin Motor Company's works at Longbridge.

Because of family circumstances, Bill was forced to leave school at the age of 14, and, wearing a pair of new blue serge trousers, which had cost 5/- (25p) he travelled to Longbridge on his bicycle to attend his first job interview at 'The Austin.'

The interview was successful, and Bill was offered an apprenticeship as a pattern maker. Fortunately he was good at woodwork at school, and so was happy with the choice of work that he was offered.

Just four months after starting his apprenticeship, Mr Ross, the Pattern Shop Foreman summoned Bill to his office. "Go to Lord Austin's office; he wants a job doing." He made the short journey down to the South Yard, passing the Drawing Office and the spares department en-route. He recalls being extremely nervous, it was quite frightening for a 14 year old country boy to be called to Lord Austin's office.

The 'Old Man's' office was located in the original White & Pike building, visible from Gate K directly opposite the traffic island where the A38 and Lickey Road separate. His office was through the main door of the building, down a passage to the bottom, and in the door on the right. Often the main door to the office was open and guarded by Austin's secretary, Bobby Howitt. Indeed, on this occasion Howitt, dressed in his customary bowler hat and spats, immediately intercepted Bill.

"What do you want?"

"Mr Ross sent me to do a little job, Sir."

"Wait here," he said sharply, and then went down the passage to speak to the 'Old Man.' After about two minutes, he called Bill down and indicated that he should enter the office.

Bill knocked on the partly open door, and stood there waiting, unable to stop himself shaking. Lord Austin looked up from his desk.

"Mr Ross sent me about the little job, Sir."

"Ah yes, come through. See the door, it will not stay open. I need a wedge for it."

Immediately that afternoon, Bill fashioned the wedge from either beech or mahogany, marking it out, band-sawing, machine-sanding and hand-finishing it with glass paper 'as though it had been planed.' The finish was left 'in the white.'

It was delivered by Bill later that afternoon, no doubt to the total satisfaction of Lord Austin.

Two years later the Luftwaffe bombed the salt works at Stoke Prior during a night-time air raid, the blast taking the roof off his mother's house. Bill recalled that the air was pungent with the smell of cordite. One of the bombs hit the railway line and lifted a section of the track complete with sleepers, one of which landed on the shed in the garden which had housed Bill's bike. It took him some hours to dig it out from the resulting mess and debris, causing him to arrive at work quite late in the morning.

"Where have you been?" Frank Ross, his boss asked.

"Been bombed, sir!"

"Did they hit the Boat?" (the local public house)

"No, sir."

"Ah, good job. Now son, make sure you get here on time in future, otherwise it's the sack for you!"

Chapter 18

TAXI!

I dare say, that had it not been for the dogged determination of young William Overton to speak personally to Sir Herbert Austin, after journeying up from London, and his absolute faith in the suitability of the Austin Twelve-Four motor car to be used as the basis for a taxicab suited to the rigours of London life, he may well have headed straight back to London on the next available train, and the taxi scene would probably have been dominated by – well, who knows? Morris, Beardmore, or any number of 'foreign' makes such as Renault, Fiat or Citroën.

As it was, William refused to leave Longbridge until he had spoken to Herbert Austin, and to put his case to him personally. After all, the Austin Twelve-Four, with taxi coachwork by the Chelsea-based Elkington Carriage Company, had proved to be very highly regarded in Manchester where Mann & Overton had deployed them.

The outcome was, as we now know, that Austin did agree to listen to him, and, furthermore, agreed to comply with his demand to modify the chassis, to ensure that it complied with Scotland Yard's Public Carriage Office's turning circle of 25ft, thus providing the capital with the finest fleet of purpose-built taxicabs the world would ever see.

The first modified 12/4 was fitted with a taxicab body by the coachbuilders Dyer & Holden, and was sold to Mr A W Barker, who was highly respected in the cab trade. He paid £380 (cash) for it, and it was licensed on 7th June, 1930. A further 271 Austin taxicabs were to be purchased that year, and over 400 in 1931.

The life of a London taxi was just

The first recorded Austin Twelve-Four taxicab modified for service in London. (Courtesy Bill Munro)

ten years, after which, having covered best part of a million miles, they were considered to be only fit for scrap. This ruling was put on hold, however, in 1939, as the start of the Second World War saw new taxicabs become impossible to obtain, and many cabs, including those approaching the end of their working life were pressed into undertaking 'war work.'

1932 'High Loader' taxicab representing those conscripted for war work between 1939 and 1945. (Courtesy Anthony Blackman)

At the outbreak of hostilities there were over 6690 cabs licensed in London, and of those, 2000 were assigned to the Auxiliary Fire Service (AFS) to serve alongside the regular fire brigade vehicles in fighting the many fires caused by enemy bombardment.

By the end of hostilities, there were less than 3000 cabs considered to be in a fit state to continue plying for hire, and, with spare parts almost non-existent, those that survived just had to soldier on as best they could.

It would be at least a further five years before new taxicabs would be ready, which saw the 'ten year' life now extending well into the 1950s, when the oldest would have been on the road for 25 years.

The Austin taxicabs had a certain charm about them, even when new they were still considered 'old-fashioned' with their artillery wheels, bulb horn, flat windscreen, open luggage platform, leather landaulet hood, and very little protection from the elements afforded to the driver – all specific requirements demanded by the Metropolitan Police.

US servicemen, still based in the UK after the War, were quick to take advantage of these 'quaint old cabs' as and when they became available, and many were shipped over to the United States as a 'souvenir' of their stay in England. Students, too, were

Three Austin 'Low Loader' taxicabs at Oxford Circus in London 1952.
(Courtesy Richard Jones, oldclassiccar.co.uk)

quick to grab them as they came off the ranks for something in the region of £30-£50, many then being pushed to the limit with epic journeys across the channel to recently liberated European countries, and, in several instances, much further afield.

One such couple, Michael and Nita Marriott, on purchasing a 1935 cab which they named 'Bertha,' decided to attempt a journey across the Sahara Desert to Kano in Nigeria. Sadly, in spite of their valiant efforts the poor old cab finally expired under

a tree at Tanout, just a couple of hundred miles from their planned destination. They wrote a graphic account of their journey in a book entitled *Desert Taxi* which is certainly

From the book
Desert Taxi Bertha is
photographed with
Nita Marriott and
members of the French
Foreign Legion at
Tammanrasset, Algeria.
(Courtesy S Gifford)

This Jones-bodied low loader ended up as a flower stall in London's Knightsbridge. (Courtesy Mike Worthington-Williams)

Two travel-weary low loaders, 'Clara' and 'Salome,' meet up at Calais after completing epic journeys abroad. (Courtesy Richard Jones, oldclassiccar.co.uk)

Back home and 'Clara' finds a new role as transport for a West London Scout troupe. (Courtesy Richard Jones, oldclassiccar.co.uk)

worth looking out for in secondhand book shops as regrettably it is no longer in print.

Another retired cab was purchased by the Bertram Mills Circus, where, painted in red and yellow, and driven around the ring by the circus clowns, no doubt provided great amusement to the younger members of the audience.

One retired taxicab, however, was a familiar sight in Knightsbridge in the late 1950s, where it did sterling work as a flower stall.

I fondly remember two such 'retired' cabs, one of which was painted to resemble a public house, complete with Watney's Red Barrel signs, whilst another was turned into a country cottage complete with flowers garden and a thatched roof.

Many of these 'old timers' sadly ended up on the scrap heap, but there were quite a few which did survive, to be restored, rebuilt or just cherished, as they were, and remain so today as a lasting reminder of London's iconic Austin taxicabs.

Prior to its continental journey, 'Clara' needed some attention to the brakes. (Courtesy Richard Jones, oldclassiccar.co.uk)

DLT 141 (actually ALE 165 – see photo on page 96), as it appeared in an episode of *Agatha Christie's Poirot.* (Courtesy Anthony Blackman, the cab's owner)

Chapter 19

The 1914 Austrian Alpine Trial

The following story was put together as a result of reading a booklet produced by The Austin Motor Company shortly after the event, and which described in detail the Trial, and the perils of driving over some of Europe's most treacherous and unforgiving roads.

It was only a matter of time before those who had invested large sums of money into the manufacture and subsequent purchase of the 'new-fangled' horseless carriages, would want to know just how fast they could go, and how reliable they were likely to be.

Mr A H Kendall and Vernon Austin seated in the Austin 20 in which they competed in the 1914 Austrian Alpine Trial. Note: The headlamps were electric, but acetylene during the Trial.
(Author's collection)

The way in which to determine both these questions was to pit one horseless carriage against another in a race or as a trial of endurance. In Britain, a race of any sort along the Queen's highway was totally out of the question, as speed was restricted at that time to a man walking in front of the vehicle waving a red flag.

However, owners of such vehicles living on the continent of Europe were much more fortunate in that respect, and, with no such restrictions imposed upon them, were able to go as fast as their vehicles could take them. In consequence, it was not long before organised road races and trials over terrain far more suited to mountain goats than motorised vehicles were taking place all over Europe.

The first such 'trial,' which ran through parts of the South Tyrol, was organised by the Austrian Touring Club in 1898. One participant was Prince Henry of Prussia, the younger brother of Kaiser Wilhelm. Henry was very different in nature to Wilhelm, and was genuinely liked by many people, unlike his brother who was completely unstable. Henry was full of enthusiasm for both motoring and yachting events and he had sufficient influence to convince prospective participants that they must compete in order to defend the honour of their county. Believing motoring events could be better organised, he took it upon himself to enlist the help of the Imperial Automobile Club of Germany, to look into the feasibility of organising a more severe test of endurance than that offered previously. The first Prinz Heinrich Fahrt took place a few years later in 1908, with another following in 1909.

By 1914, the Austrian Alpine Trial, as it then became known, was considered to be

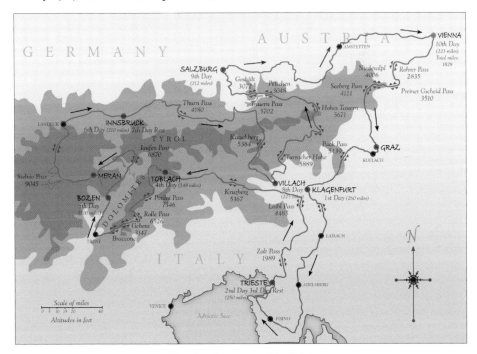

Map showing route of the Trial.

the toughest event for both man and his machine ever devised. The 1914 event was held in the June of that year, and attracted over 75 vehicles from Europe, the USA, and, of course, Great Britain, with an entry of just five motor cars, one of which was a 20hp Austin touring car entered by the Austin Motor Company, and driven by A H Kendall, AMIME, with Herbert Austin's son Vernon riding as mechanic.

Other British manufacturers also participated, and it is worth mentioning two in particular. Firstly, Rolls-Royce entered a car driven by James Radley, who put up a superb performance; the style of Rolls-Royce 40/50hp that he drove became known as the 'Alpine Eagle.' Secondly, Vauxhall Motors took up the challenge. The type of car they entered became known as a 'Prince Henry,' and historians have subsequently declared that this was the first true sports car. The well-known motoring writer Kent Karslake, said that the Vauxhall was "the first vintage and last of the veteran cars." Perhaps there may have been other significant points arising from the 'Trial' in terms of automobile development, but that is all open to speculation. With the outbreak of the Great War less than two months later, automobile manufacturers turned their attention to other more pressing matters.

Let us return to the details of the Austrian Alpine Trial, and especially to the Austin participants. Commencing on Sunday 14th June from the Austrian capital, Vienna, the eight day tour was to cover 1828 miles over some of the most gruelling roads ever encountered, and climb mountains amounting (in total) to over 107,523ft. From Vienna, the route took them south west to Klagenfurt – a total of 260 miles. On day two they travelled a further 250 miles down to Trieste. The third day was a rest day, which gave competitors the chance to relax, and plan for the days which were to follow.

On day four they drove on to Loibl, via Zolt, where heavy rain, which had fallen for some time before the event, had turned what counted as roads into muddy tracks, and where two of the passes, the Niederalpl and the Pack were reduced to nothing more than a succession of deep gullies. According to a report in *The Motor*: "The Austin in Mr Kendall's experienced hands, did the Loibl in fine style, overhauling many, and having plenty of reserve power." Their journey on that day took them through the Kruzberg passes and on to Tolbach, covering a distance of 248 miles, and attaining altitudes of 4247ft.

By this time, of the 75 cars that had started the trial in Vienna, 31 had managed

On the outward journey to Vienna. Waiting to circumvent the Arlberg Pass which had been made impassable by 12ft (3.65m) of snow.

The Austin at the commencement of the contest.

The end of the Broccone descent, saying goodbye to the Dolomites.

the course without losing any marks, but ten cars had also retired due to a number of reasons, which were mainly attributed to them being unable to manage the steepest gradients.

On day five they continued on to Bozen, a distance of 200 miles, then on through the Dolomites, climbing the 6563ft-high Fazargo Mountain, the 6950ft Pordoijoch Mountain, where a recent dam burst on a hillside had caused an avalanche of water, mud and stones making the road totally impassable – so much so that the vehicles had to use a small pathway through an orchard to bypass it, and then eventually rejoin the road further on.

Once back on the road they then climbed the 6150ft Rolle Mountain, which has a maximum gradient of 1 in 16. This took them on to the Gebera Mountain, at a mere 3147ft but with a 1 in 12 gradient, then finally through to Bozen via the Braccone Passes.

The next day saw them leave Bozen for Innsbruck, via the Jaufen Pass which had 1 in 8 gradient at some 6495ft, and the Hochfinskrmuenz Pass at 4616ft with gradients of 1 in 5.5, eventually arriving in Innsbruck after covering a further 210 miles along the way.

Day seven was another 'rest day,' but, resuming again on the eighth, they then had to travel to Villach covering a further 225 miles, during the course of which they had to negotiate the passes of Thurn, Tauernhöhe (4387ft with gradients of 1 in 4.8), and the Katschberg (5087ft, also with gradients of 1 in 4.8), during which they were timed, and where the Austin beat all its rivals in achieving the climb in just 12 minutes at a recorded speed of 61.6 miles per hour.

On the ninth and final day, they left Villach for Salzberg, a distance of 212 miles, including climbing the 3905ft Turracherhöhe mountain which contained several steep gradients. Here the organisers had engaged the use of bullocks and horses to help tow vehicles which could not make the gradient on their own, however the Austin did not require such assistance. Then on to the final leg of the trial to Vienna, another 223 miles where, thankfully, no further passes of any note were encountered.

The Trial ended with a measured five kilometre sprint along the flat, which although the Austin was driven faultlessly, was beaten by a few of the sixty remaining cars which had a larger engine capacity. However, from starting 55th, the Austin was placed 17th overall.

The Austin just before the start of the speed trial which was held on the final day.

In a telegram sent by Kendall to Herbert Austin on 26th June, he said:
"NON STOP EXCEPT FOR PETROL — *STOP* — NO SEALS BROKEN — *STOP* — FASTEST TIME ON FORMULA ON KATSCHBERG AND ON LEVEL — *STOP* — THIRD FASTEST OF ALL CARS — *STOP* — PASSED PERFECT AT EXAMINATION — *STOP*."

The Austin was considered to be a 'standard' model, but had a few modifications to ensure that it could compete on the same level as other entries, such as being fitted with Dunlop detachable wheels, colonial gears and radiator.

The trial was completed without any mechanical breakdowns, but when filling the tank with petrol in Salzburg during a severe thunderstorm, the driver was forced to stop due to water somehow getting into the petrol tank. Whilst every care was taken to ensure this did not happen by filtering the petrol into the tank through a chamois leather, somehow water did get in and 4 penalty points were awarded as a result of stopping to rectify this problem.

That the Austin 20 proved itself to be a very robust and reliable motor car, was probably best summed up by *The Bystander*, which stated "The great Austrian wrecking trials are finished, and although they do not stand alone with success, the British contingent have faced with no small credit the 'caniveau' (gullies/gutters) and hairpin bends: have encountered the rudeness of river-bed like passes: have overcome appalling ascents so steep that the cars almost required sucker tyres to keep them hanging on to the face of the mountain: and have pulled through weather that must have been made especially horrible (at times) for the occasion. They have done their part in a manner highly creditable to the British motor industry. The Austin in particular drew general admiration all round."

Although the 1914 Austrian Alpine Trial was won by a 14/45 Type 'C' Audi, driven by August Horch, it can safely be said that the new Austin 20 was proved to be an exceptionally good motor car. Regrettably, due to certain events that kicked off just a couple of months later because of an incident which occurred in a city not all that far away from where the Trial took place, the motoring public would have to wait at least another five years before they could buy one for themselves.

Whilst the British press, without exception, hailed the British entries, and especially that of the Austin as being quite outstanding, the German motoring magazine *Allgemeine Automobil-Zeitung* was not so praiseworthy. In fact, if you take the contents of their article at face value, it would lead you to believe that the Austin Motor Company, in their booklet about this event did not tell it exactly how it was. The translated text of the article reads as follows:

We came across an edition of the English *Car* magazine from 12th December last year, in which we found an advert from the English Austin Motor Company, which was written and composed in rhymes. The English advertising poet sings of/ praises the Austin in truly enthusiastic manner. We find out from this poem that an Austin car has been THE Alpine hero of 1914. Each stanza of the hymn finishes with the refrain: "Austin! Famed Victor! The Alpine Hero!" As the bard seemed to be concerned the reader might not be fully convinced of the fame of the Austin through his poetry alone, he added some prose which we are repeating below: "Shortly before the beginning of the war a 20hp Austin competed in the Austrian Alpine Race and won the great silver medal." The correspondent of *The Motor* writes: "The Austin showed its outstanding performance on the Katschberg, that famous ascending slope. Not a single car of any other make was able to show such a glowing record, not even one of those which cost twice as much as the Austin. Within less than four weeks, the Austin covered 7800 miles unaided, ie, the Alpine Race as well as the trip from and back to England. During that time, the Austin managed to tackle 40 mountain passes with a combined height of 120,000ft without a single mechanical stop and without any pneumatic damage."

Austin, the famed victor, the alpine hero ... We decided to research the official results of the Alpine Race of 1914, and found the famous Austin with the start number of 55 managed to 'achieve' 14 first class penalty points during the eight stages of the race. At this point, it has to be mentioned that there were five assessment categories designed for the Alpine Race of 1914: no penalty points, third class penalty points, second class penalty points, first class penalty points, and penalty points from more than one class. According to that, first class penalty points were directly following the very worst still classified category, ie, the one with penalty points from more than one class. The Great Silver Medal which the Austin won according to *Car*, is in fact reduced to a silver sticker, once you have studied the official results of the Alpine Race of 1914, and the silver sticker was given to every car "which had managed to reach each stage before the deadline."

According to *Car*, the Austin, the "Famed Victor, The Alpine Hero" has managed to cover 7000 miles (the author seems to have knocked off 800 miles at this point, it actually totalled 11,263km) including the Alpine race, without a single mechanical stop. To illustrate/look closer at this claim, it has to be mentioned that first class penalty points, of which the Austin had 14, were punishment for the following: 1, One penalty point for each commenced minute of an involuntary stop; 2, One point for each commenced minute more than the allowed ten minutes maintenance time at the beginning; 3, Five penalty points for breaking a seal during a stage, even if no repair was carried out; 4, Ten penalty points for adding cooling liquid during a stage; 5, Three penalty points for each commenced minute of stopping or rolling back on one of the valley routes, which are marked by starting and finishing tape; 6, One penalty point for each commenced per cent more than ten per cent above the allowed time for completing the performance assessment stretches.

The educated reader can now make his own judgement on what to think about the claim from *Car* that the Austin was able to finish the Alpine race without a single mechanical stop, and that should give you the true picture of the Hero Austin of the Alpine Race 1914. The only true remark is that the Austin was able to undercut its personal maximum permissible time by more than any other contestant on the performance assessment stretch on the Katschberg. Admittedly, the best time was achieved by an Englishman, however not by the driver of the Austin, but by a certain Mr Radley who managed to drive a large Rolls-Royce within 7 minutes and 18 seconds across the Katschberg stretch, which had a length of 5km and 700 metres, and ascending slopes of up to 23% had to be mastered. On those stretches the large and heavy cars were disadvantaged by their personal maximum permissible time, compared with the lighter cars. Therefore it is correct, as mentioned above, that the Austin managed to undercut its personal maximum permissible time – which was 24 minutes and 30 seconds – more than any other car; it only needed 11 minutes and 58 seconds, ie: undercut the time by 12 minutes and 32 seconds. However, an almost equally good result was achieved by the Hansa Wagen, driven by Loeller, which undercut its maximum permissible time by 12 minutes and 12 seconds, as well as Robert Koch in his Opel with 10 minutes and 33 seconds.

It can certainly not be claimed that the Austin was the hero of the Alpine Race 1914 or that it won the Great Silver medal. A car, which collected 14 first class penalty points, whereas 19 of its opponents remained without any penalty points, must not be sung of as "Austin! Famed Victor! The Alpine Hero!" Such exploitation of the participation in a motoring competition for an advertisement, especially when the competition had been run by a country with which they are currently at war, shows a lack of the 'fair play' that the English are always emphasising when it comes to sporting events.

Thus reads the text from the *Allgemeine Automobil-Zeitung*, written several months after the event, and when both Germany and England were at war with each other. Sour grapes, or a true account of the Austin's participation in the 1914 Austrian Alpine Trial ? We will probably never quite know the truth, but, given how 'traditionally' adverts have always tended to highlight the good points of a product and perhaps gloss over or even omit the bad, then it is up to the reader to make up his own mind on this.

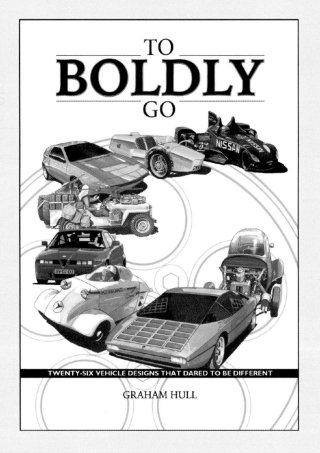

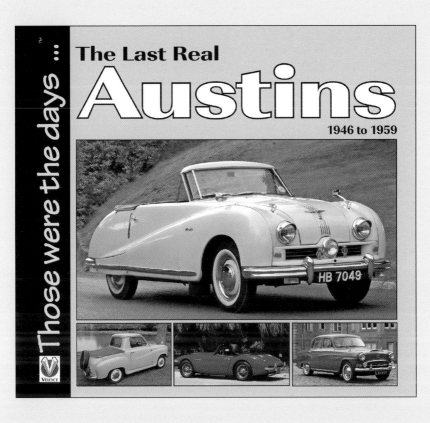

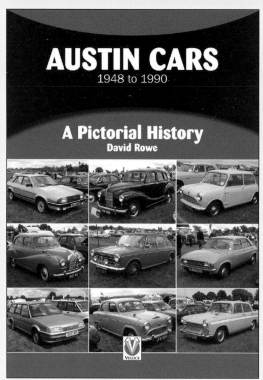
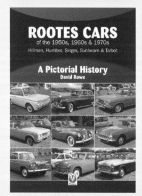
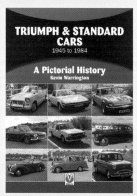
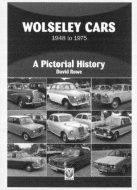

INDEX